FIRST
COMES LOVE

FIRST COMES LOVE

Finding Your Family in the Church and the Trinity

SCOTT HAHN

DOUBLEDAY

New York • London • Toronto • Sydney • Auckland

PUBLISHED BY DOUBLEDAY
a division of Random House, Inc.
1540 Broadway, New York, New York 10036

DOUBLEDAY and the portrayal of an anchor with a dolphin are trademarks of
Doubleday, a division of Random House, Inc.

Book design by Julie Duquet

Library of Congress Cataloging-in-Publication Data
Hahn, Scott.
First comes love: finding your family in the church and the Trinity /
by Scott Hahn.—1st ed.
p. cm.
Includes bibliographical references.
1. Family—Religious aspects—Catholic Church. 2. Catholic Church—Doctrines.
3. Trinity. 4. Church. I. Title.
BX2351.H34 2002
261.8'3585—dc21
2001032320

Nihil Obstat: Rev. James Dunfee, Censor Librorum

Imprimatur: Most Reverend Gilbert Sheldon, Bishop of Steubenville,
December 19, 2001

The *Nihil Obstat* and *Imprimatur* are official declarations that a book or pamphlet is
free of doctrinal or moral error. No implication is contained therein that those who
have granted the *Nihil Obstat* and *Imprimatur* agree with the contents, opinions or
statements expressed.

To Michael Scott Hahn

CONTENTS

FOREWORD
By Ronald D. Lawler, O.F.M. Cap.
Member, Pontifical Roman Theological Academy

T HIS BOOK RINGS with great ideas, drawn from Scripture, from the Fathers, and from the lived faith of the Church, to help us know how great and good God is, by seeing how He has created small human families and the great family of faith as images of the deepest and dearest mystery, the mystery of God Himself.

God is great, and He is full of love. He is not a solitary God. He does not tower above heaven and earth as one entirely alone. He is a Father, and He has an eternal Son, to Whom He is united with dearest closeness by the love that is the Holy Spirit. He is a family.

Because He is great, God wishes His children to be great and to be filled with love. As the eternal Father is forever a member of the divine family we call the Trinity, He is not alone, and He cries out from the beginning of mankind that "it is not good that the man should be alone" (Gn 2:18). We are to live in love and in families—in our own little families, in the family of faith, and in the family of the Trinity.

Human persons are called to live in great love, in families. A man and a woman are called to find the love that overcomes the deep loneliness and selfishness our flesh can be heir to, by giving themselves entirely to each other in the love that creates marriage and homes and calls into being children more dear to parents than all else.

Human love is weak, and human families need to be caught into the great family of God to become what they long to be. Even before God taught us fully the mystery of the Trinity, He called the first man to find God as his Father, to live as God's son, and to do for his Father the familial tasks of tilling the earth and guarding it.

The first head of the human family failed, so God made known and sent to us His eternal Son, to bring to us in a more sublime way the gifts of love and unity He wished us to have. Cardinal Newman speaks of how what failed in Adam most surely did not fail in Christ.

O loving wisdom of our God!
When all was sin and shame,
A second Adam to the fight
And to the rescue came.

O wisest love! that flesh and blood
Which did in Adam fail,
Should strive afresh against the foe,
Should strive and should prevail.

And that a higher gift than grace
Should flesh and blood refine,
God's Presence and His very Self
And Essence all-divine.

This book begins with the story of that first Adam and returns to his story again and again, in a spiral fashion, examining the Genesis narrative in light of the second Adam, Jesus Christ. In Christ, our small human families are to be caught into the sublime family of God and know with the warmth of faith that God is indeed their Father. But our families are to be caught also into the great family visible about us, more blessed and saving than any of the "trustee families" of antiquity (see chapter 2). Our families are to be caught into the family of the Church. For the Church both mirrors that Family of God, which is the Trinity, and *is* on earth the Family of God, which gives constant encouragement and gifts of life to small families.

Astonishingly striking are the ways in which the mystery of the human family and the mightier mystery of the Family of God are brought into unity by Jesus, the eternal Son. The place of the Eucharist is spoken of with great fire here (chapter 7). When Adam failed to show the love God enabled him to share, and led his human family into sin, the eternal Son became our very brother and the new head and founder of our human family, and He did not fail. He gave us, and all in our families, kinship with God. As Dr. Hahn puts it: "Our kinship with God is so real that His very blood courses through our bodies. . . . In the New Covenant meal, the Family of God eats the body of Christ and so *becomes* the body of Christ. . . . 'The children share in flesh and blood' (Heb 2:14)."

The book draws to a close with a treasury of "Sources and References," whose riches I urge you to consult.

In the visible family of the Church, as in the family of the Trinity that is God, every person, however broken his or her home and hopes may have been, can find a most dear family. The Church offers strength and light to every small family—that it may with gladness and greatness become what it is made to be: a place of love, shining with the gifts of the God Who enables the family and each of its members to acquire varying and wonderful kinds of greatness.

Every family, even the weakest and most suffering family, is called to greatness. And it can come to greatness, for it is meant to be, and can be, caught into the great Family of God Himself, Who is the source and joy of greatness for all.

CHAPTER 1

THE OLDEST STORY
IN THE WORLD

F EW ARE THE powers that can lure a college student away from his cafeteria. The undergraduate male sustains an enormous and primal appetite for food—even institutional food. And I was as undergraduate and as male as any other student at Grove City College.

Yet, one autumn day, I discovered a force of nature that trumps even food. Her name was Kimberly Kirk.

I spied her playing piano just outside the dining hall. The music was beautiful, but music—even at its finest, and her songs *were* dazzling—ranks relatively low with the undergraduate male.

At a distance, I could see that the young woman at the keyboard had a cute, sassy haircut—and a sassier smile.

I made my way over and, between songs, tried to make casual conversation. She was, I found out, very active in theater and interested in literature; her major was communication arts. She played a piece she had written, and it was magnificent. Then she sang to her own accompaniment, and I thought to myself, *She could do this for a living.*

I knew I had better move on, and quickly. Scott Hahn was not about to fall for another woman. You see, not too long before that encounter, I had made a firm decision to quit dating. After several relationships, I concluded that the dating scene was an emotional trap, an extended battery of mind games—hurting and getting hurt. I'd had enough. Besides, I was already triple-majoring in economics, philosophy, and theology, and working as a resident assistant. I just didn't have the time.

So, that autumn day, with a polite "Nice to meet you," I turned my undergraduate-student body back toward the cafeteria.

My mind, however, was another matter. A few days later, I was walking across the quad and I caught sight of Kimberly Kirk a half-quad away. Watching her walk, I thought, *Boy, is she pretty.* Then I thought back to our encounter in the dining hall: *And she's really intelligent and musical . . .*

Still, my stubborn will remained. I couldn't ask her for a date. Dating was out of the question at that point in my life—even dating a young woman so radiantly beautiful, so witty, and so talented. No, I couldn't do it.

So I did the next-best thing. I asked her if she would consider joining me in Young Life, a youth-ministry program I was helping to run at a local high school. She said yes, to my delight, never letting on to me that her dad had been one of the founding leaders of Young Life, some two decades before!

In this shared ministry, I really *saw* Kimberly Kirk. She had faith and an evangelical zeal that surpassed all her other gifts. I never tired of her company. Soon we were spending four, five, six hours a day together, punctuating our work with snowball fights, long walks, long conversations, and music, sweet music.

Within a month, my rash vow had expired. I was a goner. Kimberly Kirk and I were falling in love.

I don't mean to bore you with personal details. I know that there's nothing exceptional about our story. We met; we were attracted to one another, yet determined to tough it out alone; so we resisted the attraction till we could resist it no more. Boy meets girl: It's quite literally the oldest story in the world.

One Is the Loneliest Number

When Christians and Jews tell the story of the human race, they begin "in the beginning," with God's creation of a man named Adam. "Adam" is the name of an individual, the founding father of the human race, but it is more, too. *Adam* is the Hebrew word for "humanity." This is something like the way Americans use the name "Washington" to mean the first president of their country, the capital city of their country, and the government of their country. Washington's story is, in a sense, America's story. Yet Adam's story is even greater than that. It belongs to all the nations of the world and to everyone. Adam's story is our story: mine and Kimberly's, and yours.

Let's revisit that story at the beginning of the Bible. The Book of Genesis begins with the account of God's creation of the universe. In six consecutive "days," God created everything: night and day; the sky and the seas; the sun, the moon, and the stars; the birds and the fish; and the beasts of the fields. After each act of creation, God looked at what He had made and pronounced it "good." To crown His work, God created man on the sixth day and gave him dominion over all the earth. Only then did God look at His work and declare it "very good" (Gn 1:31).

We see in the next chapter of Genesis that God furnished the whole world for man's delight. "And out of the ground the Lord God made to grow every tree that is pleasant to the sight and good for food" (2:9). God gave Adam this lush, fruitful garden to till and to keep (2:15). Thus, Adam lived in a world custom-made for his pleasure, a world without sin, suffering, or disease—a world where work was always rewarding, a world that, Genesis tells us, was unstintingly *good*.

Yet God Himself looked upon this situation and, for

the first time in the Scriptures, pronounced that something was "not good." He said, "It is not good that the man should be alone" (Gn 2:18).

What a remarkable statement! Remember, this took place before the Fall of humankind, before sin and disorder could enter creation. Adam lived in an earthly paradise as a child of God, made in God's own image (Gn 1:27). Yet something was "not good." Something was incomplete. The man was lonely.

God set out immediately to remedy the situation, saying, "I will make him a helper fit for him" (Gn 2:18). So God brought all the animals to man and asked him to name them—to exercise authority over them.

Even so, things were still "not good": "for the man there was not found a helper fit for him" (Gn 2:20). Though Adam could rule over the beasts—though he could enjoy fruitful, rewarding labor—he was still unfulfilled. For God made man on the same day as the animals, but He made man different from the animals. Only man was made in God's image and likeness. Thus, even with all the animals in the world, man was alone upon the earth.

What comes next in Genesis is the heart of every love story:

"So the Lord God caused a deep sleep to fall upon the man, and while he slept took one of his ribs and closed up its place with flesh; and the rib which the Lord God had taken from the man He made into a woman and brought her to the man. Then the man said: 'This at last is bone of my bones and flesh of my flesh; she shall be called Woman, because she was taken out of Man'" (2:21–23).

Adam's world had seemed complete. He had a good job, a beautiful home, dutiful pets, and plenty to keep him busy. Yet he was incomplete. Even as the "image of God," he was only complete when the woman, Eve, joined him in life. The man and his wife became "one flesh" (Gn 2:24). "So God created man in His own image, in the image of God He created him; male and female He created them" (Gn 1:27).

Adam should never have known loneliness again, because he had Eve by his side in a perfect world. He could see, now, that there was more to life than fruitful labor, more to life than a beautiful house, more to life than power. There was truly human love. Nor would Adam's good company be limited to the perfect match, the "helper fit for him." For "God blessed them, and God said to them, 'Be fruitful and multiply, and fill the earth'" (Gn 1:28).

The image of God was made complete with the creation of the family. Only then was Eden truly paradise.

From Garden to Grove

Boy meets girl. Adam meets Eve. Scott meets Kimberly. You know the story. It's the stuff of most of our movies, novels, ancient epics, and popular songs. It's the substance of our fondest memories, our deepest longings, or our most aching needs. It is not good to be alone.

Whenever I read this oldest story in the world, I can't help but get nostalgic, and I can't help but identify with Adam. I had all that I thought I needed in life: three academic majors, each of which I found fascinating; an active and rewarding ministry with young people; and, of course, a cafeteria. I lived on a treelined campus that was pleasant to the sight, stimulating to the mind, and generous at mealtimes. I didn't even know I was incomplete—I couldn't know—until I saw what I'd been missing.

God had made me not just for philosophy, economics, theology, or ministry, as good as all these things might be. God had created me for much more than that, and God had created me for Kimberly Kirk. His image in me would not begin to be complete until I said yes to His clear calling for me to marry her.

God made me, as He made you and everyone else on earth, for family. All the things we see and hear and feel and taste in creation are *good,* but it is *not good* for us to be alone.

What I'll call the family imperative is a basic assumption in our culture. Universities know it, for example, and so they try to market themselves as a surrogate family to teens who are making their first venture from the parental homestead. They succeed remarkably well, creating bonds that often last a lifetime. The college I attended likes to refer to itself in alumni mailings as *alma mater,* which is Latin for "nourishing mother." The campus has both fraternities and sororities—literally, *brotherhoods* and *sisterhoods*—and every year it celebrates *homecoming* week. The folks at the alumni association know that, as long as they can keep those family associations alive, I'm more likely to send money "home" to Grove City College.

Not Your Garden-Variety Families

Marketers know it, and we know it, too. We are made for family. For many people, this is a self-evident truth; but for some, it is an empty or broken promise, an almost unbelievable proposition. In recent generations, we have seen the family, as an institution, fall into rapid decline. A century ago, most marriages ended only with the death of a spouse. Today, many marriages end, bitterly, in divorce. Many children must come to terms with feelings of abandonment by one or both parents. Many adults struggle with anger and a deep sense of betrayal. Family dysfunction is epidemic, if not pandemic.

For the victims of such circumstances, the word "family" does not evoke happy memories or pleasant associations. For them, it seems a cruel God who would create us to live amid treachery, unkindness, or even abuse.

Those who have grown up in dysfunctional homes, or those who have been betrayed by lovers, know that they have been deprived of *some great good*. Their anger, bitterness, and sadness overwhelm them precisely because they know they lack *something essential*. They have been deprived of *something that is theirs by right*. They nurse a deep wound, and a wound is the sign that something in nature has been pierced, cut, or broken.

The wound is a sign that they lacked something that a family should have provided. Their family was not what it should have been, not what God created it to be. The fault, then, is not with the family as God created it, but with particular families as they stray from God's plan. Family dysfunction is undoubtedly a consequence of Original Sin; but it is *not* something God dreamed up to torment us.

Indeed, our only hope for regaining wholeness and happiness is if we recover God's family plan for creation. The *Catechism of the Catholic Church* (CCC) tells us that we must all "cleanse our hearts" of any "false . . . paternal or maternal images, stemming from our personal and cultural history, and influencing our relationship with God. God our Father transcends the categories of the created world. To impose our own ideas in this area 'upon Him' would be to fabricate idols to adore or pull down. To pray to the Father is to enter into His mystery as He is and as the Son has revealed Him to us" (no. 2779).

We must make the effort to undergo this cleansing, because God's family plan is more than just a recipe for domestic order (though it is that, too). It is a fulfillment of our deepest longings: for love, for family, for home. It is a recovery of the romance we were made to enjoy . . . forever. More than that, it is the title deed to a family estate that no one, not even the tax collector, can take from us. Still more, it is the revelation of God Himself, in His deepest mystery.

For at the core of human experience is the family, which is familiar to all of us, and which most of us think we understand, while somewhere far beyond the limits of our minds is God the Blessed Trinity, Whom many people find remote, abstract, and inaccessible. Yet I propose that we *don't* understand what we think we understand—that is, the family—and we *do* possess a key to understanding what we find inscrutable: the Trinity.

Labor Union

I believe all this because I have seen it. I married Kimberly Kirk on August 18, 1979. We made our home, and we knew the pleasure and the joy of the union of a man and a woman. It was not, however, in the ecstasy of our bodily union that I first glimpsed how a family most vividly manifests God's life—though that union surely had something to do with it.

For me, the first revelation came when Kimberly was nine and a half months pregnant with our first child. Her body had taken on new proportions, and more than ever before I realized that her flesh was not created merely for my delight. What I had enjoyed as something beautiful was now becoming a means to a greater end.

When she felt her first labor pains, we rushed to the hospital with the anticipation that our baby would soon be in our arms. Kimberly's labor was difficult, however, right from the start. I joked that if men could get pregnant, the human race would have been extinct soon after its creation.

The hours dragged on, hours of hard labor, and Kimberly's pain grew more intense. My heart gave lie to my joking, because I would gladly have taken on her pain at that moment.

We passed a day this way, and then a night, and then another day began. After thirty hours of labor, the doctor saw little progress, and he recommended a cesarean section. This was not at all the way we had wanted things to go, but we saw that the choice was being taken out of our hands.

Exhausted, I watched the nurses move Kimberly to a gurney and wheel her down the hall to another room. I walked alongside, holding her hand, praying with her and telling jokes—anything to lift her spirit.

When we arrived at the operating room, the nurses moved Kimberly again, now to a table, where they strapped her down and sedated her. She was freezing cold, shivering, and afraid.

I stood beside my wife, her body spread out and strapped cruciform to the table, cut open in order to bring new life to the world.

Nothing my dad had told me about the facts of life, nothing I had learned in high school biology class, could have prepared me for that moment. The doctors allowed me to stay, to watch the operation. As the surgeon made his incisions, I beheld all of Kimberly's major organs. "Truly," I thought, "we are fearfully and wonderfully made!" Then came the moment when, from amid those organs, with a few careful movements of the doctor's hands, came the beautiful body of my baby boy, my first-born son, Michael.

But it was Kimberly's body that became something *more* than beautiful for me. Bloody and scarred and swollen with pain, it became something sacred, a living temple, a holy sanctuary, and an altar of life-giving sacrifice.

The life she gave to our world—this life we had made with God—I could now look upon and touch with my hands. A third person had entered the intimate unity of our home. This was the beginning of something new for me, and for Kimberly and me together. God had taken two starry-eyed lovers' gazes and redirected them—but they were no less starry-eyed and no less loving. Now there were three in a happy home, whose love kept leading them to a home still happier.

God knows, it is not good for us to be alone. He doesn't want us to be alone. It's the oldest story in the world, and it's written into our very human nature: He wants us home.

CHAPTER 2

ADAM'S FAMILY VALUES

IT MAY SEEM self-evident that people naturally tend to live in families and that it's not good for man to be alone. Even the personal ads in the daily paper bear witness to these principles. So why should anyone write a book on the subject? And why should you read a book about it?

Because there's a lot we have to *un*learn before we can truly understand what the ancient Jews and Christians meant by family. What, after all, was the sort of family we were created for? What kind of love, and what kind of home, constitute our deepest needs? The answers to these questions might help us to see why so many people are unfulfilled in love and why so many look for love in all the wrong places.

What does the Bible mean by family? It's not what you might think.

To most of us, family means (at least in some ideal sense) "mom, dad, and the kids." Family is that closely knit group of people related by marriage or by blood and sharing a common home. A family is what fits into a suburban house or an urban apartment. Some of us would extend the bond a little further, to include cousins and any living grandparents or great-grandparents. Still others might stretch the idea of family to include second cousins. This is what modern Americans call the extended family—all the people who show up for family reunions. I often ask my university students how many of them belong to an extended family. Usually around a quarter of the people in class will raise their hands. I then ask what they mean by "extended"—how many people? The answers usually come in around thirty or forty, though some have ranged as high as five hundred.

Yet even this top number is minuscule when measured against the biblical notion of family.

The Tribal Belt

In ancient Israel—indeed, in most ancient cultures—the large, extended family defined the world of a given individual. One's family included all the descendants of a given patriarch, usually a man who lived centuries before. The nation of Israel itself was such a family, since it was populated mostly by those who claimed descent from the patriarch Jacob (also known as Israel). Jacob's twelve sons, in turn, provided the family identity for the "Twelve Tribes" of Israel. Each tribe, then, was a distinct family whose members called one another "brothers" and "sisters," children of a common father, the long-ago patriarch. So even distant cousins were considered siblings. In fact, most ancient Semitic languages had no word for "cousin," since "brother" or "sister" served the purpose. In the Old Testament Book of Joshua, we see a vivid depiction of this social arrangement, with tribes, clans, and households roughly corresponding to our modern ideas of federal, state, and municipal government. "So Joshua . . . brought Israel near tribe by tribe, and the tribe of Judah was taken; and he brought near the families of Judah, and the family of the Zerahites was taken; and he brought near the family of the Zerahites man by man, and Zabdi was taken; and he brought near his household man by man" (7:16–18).

Often, the tribal family was bound by inheritance to a certain parcel of land. Thus, the "Land of Judah" (Judea) was the home of the descendants of Judah. The land was their patrimony, received from their ancestors, which the current generation kept in trust for future generations of the family. The family identified itself with the land; to sell the family's estate was unthinkable—and sometimes legally impossible (see Lv 25:23–34).

Personal mobility, then, was also limited. One ordinarily lived and worked within the confines of one's tribal land and died in the land in which he was born. If someone did wander from the ancestral lands, he continued to identify himself with his tribe, and, throughout his life, his "home" remained the ancestral lands, and *not* the land to which he had emigrated. Moreover, his descendants would inherit this sense, considering themselves "strangers in a strange land," even in the land of their birth.

An Heir-Raising Experience

Nor did family membership end with death. Ancestors were revered in ancient cultures. Reverence was owed especially, but not exclusively, to the patriarch. The tomb of one's forebears was considered a second home. Through oral tradition, families carefully preserved their genealogies, which bridged the generations and united today's children with the patriarch.

Family members lived by a code, usually unwritten, that dictated their duties within the clan and their behavior toward those outside the clan. All members were bound to uphold the family's honor. A man did not choose a trade based on his interests or even his skills; his work was determined by the family's need, and his earnings were accumulated for the family's benefit.

Ultimately, one's family membership defined one's religion. The family was a religious community above all, perpetuated for the worship of its particular "household gods." Priesthood was passed from father to son (ideally the firstborn), who conducted worship according to the tradition of the ancestors. A family's god was the god of its ancestors. The Israelites, for example, knew the Lord God as "the God of Abraham and of Isaac and of Jacob, the God of our fathers" (Acts 3:13; see also Mt 22:32; Mk 12:26; Lk 20:37). This was true not only of the Israelites but also of most of the peoples of the earth, in the ancient Near Eastern lands, in ancient Greece and Rome, in India, Japan, China, and throughout Africa.

Religion in ancient civilizations was largely a local phenomenon, a family matter. More than the bonds of blood, it was this common worship that united a family across many generations and many degrees of relation. To marry into a family meant to accept that family's religious duties. To live outside the family, to move away from one's ancestral lands, to refuse to live by the family's code, meant to be cut off from the family's worship—and thus the family's life.

Putting on Heirs

Yet the door did not only open outward. A family could and did accept outsiders into full membership—but only after they had become insiders. And the legal, ritual means of welcoming new family members was through a "covenant." Covenant was an ancient family's way of extending the duties and privileges of kinship to another individual or group. When a family welcomed new members, through marriage or some other alliance, both parties—the new members and the established tribe—would seal the covenant bond, usually by solemnly swearing a sacred oath, sharing a common meal, and offering a sacrifice.

Some covenants even extended to unite two large tribal families for mutual support and protection. Yet the covenant was more than a treaty, and the covenantal parties were more than allies. By the force of the covenant, they were united as family. The great biblical scholar Dennis J. McCarthy, S.J., wrote that "the covenant between Israel and Yahweh did in fact make Israel the family of Yahweh in a very real sense. . . . the result of . . . the covenant was thought of as a kind of familial relationship."

Model Homes

Social scientists have developed many models for understanding this family arrangement. The one I've found most useful is that of Carle C. Zimmerman of Harvard University, who spoke of ancient families as "trustee families."

In his monumental work *Family and Civilization,* Zimmerman explained: "The trustee family is so named because it more or less considers itself as immortal, existing in perpetuity, and never being extinguished. As a result, the living members are not the family, but merely 'trustees' of its blood, rights, property, name, and position for their lifetime."

The trustee family envisions the family primarily in religious terms. It's not the nuclear family, or even the extended family, but all the members of the family in the past and the future as well as in the present generation. A sacred bond unites members in the present generation with the ancestors who gave them life; the same bond unites them with their future descendants, who will perpetuate the family name, honor, and worship.

This is hardly what most folks today mean when they speak of the family. Modern households tend to fall under Zimmerman's categories of the "domestic family" or the "atomistic family." The *domestic family* describes a household based on the marital bond: husband, wife, and their children. In such an arrangement, family members emphasize individual rights along with family duties. In *atomistic families,* however, individual rights are exalted far above family bonds, and the family itself exists for the sake of the individual's pleasure.

There are many remarkable differences in these historical stages. In trustee-family societies, the family is seen as a mystical reality; in domestic-family societies, it is a moral tradition; when the atomistic family dominates, the home is seen as a sort of cocoon, something you're born into in order to escape. In trustee societies, marriage is a sacred covenant; in domestic, it's a contract; in the atomistic household, it's a convenient means of companionship. Children in the trustee family are considered a blessing from the gods; in domestic, they're indispensable economic agents; in the atomistic family, however, they become an economic liability, an "expense," and an obstacle to personal fulfillment. In the trustee family, the father is the patriarch, a priest-king who must serve his ancestors as well as his offspring; in the domestic family, the father is the authoritarian chief executive of society's fundamental economic unit; in the atomistic family, he is a pathetic figure who must be left behind in order for an individual to grow. And each type of family views sexual immorality differently. For the trustee family, it's a criminal act; for the domestic, it's an individual sin; for the atomistic family, it's a private matter, a choice, an alternative lifestyle.

Zimmerman points out that only societies based on the trustee family have been able to rise to the level of civilizations. Yet none of these societies were able to maintain the trustee arrangement forever. At some point in the history of every civilization, its people begin to live according to the domestic-family model. The period of domestic-family dominance, though, is usually short-lived, a transitional phase before the atomistic family takes its place. When the atomistic family becomes a society's dominant model, then family duties are widely viewed as impediments to individual fulfillment. The atomistic family—marked by widespread divorce, unrestrained sexual activity, and population decline—usually signifies a civilization in its ultimate decline.

National Family Planning

All of this is just to help us understand what the people of ancient Israel—and Jesus Christ, and the early Christians— meant when they spoke of matters closest to their hearts and our own. We must take care, after all, not to project our modern notions onto the biblical authors' words. Family, society, and religion were, to a great extent, interchangeable for Israelites. Family trust was synonymous with religious worship, and the "family unit" was the society itself!

Thus, if you counted yourself among the sons and daughters of Israel, you numbered your "brothers and sisters" in the tens of thousands, or hundreds of thousands, or millions.

This is certainly a long stretch from God's observation that "it is not good that the man should be alone." Yet we can see the logic of the trustee family even in God's first command to the first family: "Be fruitful and multiply, and fill the earth."

It is not enough for man to be created "good." Nor, it seems, is it enough for him to have "a helper fit for him." Romance—great as it may be—is apparently not sufficient to satisfy these creatures, to fulfill their duties before God, or to complete the image of God on earth. Romance suffices, in a limited way, to take a man outside himself. Children suffice to draw a loving couple beyond their starry-eyed mutual gaze.

Yet it seems that God built us all to live in a much larger family, to experience a much larger love . . . a love that extends infinitely.

CHAPTER 3

THE FIRST CHRISTIAN
REVOLUTION

ONLY WITH A clear understanding of Jesus'
"family language" can we begin to understand
His saving message. For, throughout the
Gospels, this is the language He uses to describe His mission, His commands, His relations with God and with
others, His legacy, and His Church.

Family terminology—words such as *father, son, brother,
sister, mother, children, home, firstborn, inheritance, marriage,*
and *birth*—dominates Jesus' speech. Moreover, it dominates the writings of His first followers: St. Peter, St.
Paul, St. John, and other authors of the Scriptures. It's
not that Jesus and the early Christians had no other religious vocabulary at their disposal. Both Jesus and St.
Paul, for example, freely chose religious metaphors from
other areas of society: agriculture, sports, law, military,
even children's games.

Overwhelmingly, though, the language they came

back to—especially when they spoke of Christianity's central ideas—was the language of family.

More Than Just Friends

Nowhere is this so striking as in Jesus' descriptions of His relationship to God, Whom He dared to call "Father." For Jesus, God is not "father" in a metaphorical sense. Nor is God "father" to Jesus merely through the act of creation. On the contrary, Jesus' sonship is something real, unique, and personal (see CCC, no. 240). God, to Jesus Christ, is "Abba"—which means "Daddy" or "Papa" (see Mk 14:36).

Now, to us in the twenty-first century, this idea might not seem subversive or even very fresh. Today, the "fatherhood of God" is something freely professed not only by Christians but even by Freemasons, Unitarians, and deists. It has become part of our cultural wallpaper, a "safe" metaphor for politicians to evoke at interfaith gatherings. The idea probably reached the depths of banality during my teen years, when the bubblegum group the Archies sang, "We're just one big family, and our Daddy's in the sky."

Yet the idea was not always so common. Indeed, the ancients approached God's fatherhood only with extreme caution. In Israel, the Twelve Tribes understood themselves collectively to be the "Family of God," but in something more than a metaphorical sense, because God created them, guided them, protected them, and provided for them—as a father begets, guides, protects, and provides for his family. God, then, acted as a father to the nation of Israel (see Dt 32:6; Jer 31:9). Individually, however, Israelites tended to refer to themselves not as God's children, but as His "servants" or "slaves" (see, for example, 1 Sm 3:9 and Ps 116:16). Even the greatest of the patriarchs, Abraham, could be called God's "friend" (Is 41:8), but not His son.

This is a far cry from the popular piety of modern America. Thus, it is difficult for us to imagine the reaction of Jesus' contemporaries when He claimed to be the Son of God. That, they said, was either madness or blasphemy. In fact, that outrageous claim was precisely the reason He was arrested, tried, and executed. "This was why the Jews sought all the more to kill Him, because He . . . called God His own Father" (Jn 5:18).

The Son Also Rises

What Jesus proposed was a revolution in religious thought—occurring on two levels simultaneously. First: Here was a man, created by God, claiming an unprecedented close familial relationship with the creator. "I and the Father are one" (Jn 10:30). "He who has seen Me has seen the Father" (Jn 14:9). "I am in the Father and the Father [is] in Me" (Jn 14:10). Jesus' disciples believed His claim, and their agreement was the essence of their faith: "You are the Christ," Simon Peter told Jesus, "the Son of the living God" (Mt 16:16).

Now, this was already a mighty claim, but it implied even more. If Jesus was the Son of God and was "one" with God, He was also, in some sense, "equal with God" (Jn 5:18 again), as the son is the heir of the father. Yet, if God is one—as both Israel and Jesus maintained—how could God have an equal? Wouldn't that make Him . . . *two*?

God's equal, after all, could only be *God,* equally powerful, equally eternal, equally wise. Thus, implied in Jesus' claim of sonship is a further claim of divinity. Which brings us to His second and more profoundly revolutionary teaching.

If Jesus is equal to God, then He is God; and if God is still one, then God is also somehow a plurality. He is Father and Son—and, as Jesus would further reveal, God is Holy Spirit. God is a Trinity of persons, united as one.

These two revolutions in religious thought—that a man can be a child of God and that God is a Trinity—constitute the core doctrine of Christianity. Jesus revealed both teachings exclusively in the language of the family, and the theology of Jesus Christ is inconceivable in any but familial terms. Apart from family language, there would be no revolution, there would be no Christianity.

All in the Family

Jesus' claim of divine sonship scandalized the religious establishment in His country. The clergy considered it ample evidence to have Him convicted and executed for blasphemy. Still, there was more to His message. His mission revealed the truth not only about His own nature and His Father's but also about humankind. This truth, too, took shape in family language.

Jesus spoke of His own sonship in unique terms. He alone was the eternal Son of God. Yet He also encouraged everyone to consider God a Father. "Pray to your Father Who is in secret; and your Father Who sees in secret will reward you" (Mt 6:6). Note that He speaks not of the corporate prayer of Israel, but of private prayer. God was Father, then, to each person.

Consider, too, the words that Jesus held up as the model prayer for all disciples: "Pray then like this: Our Father Who art in heaven, hallowed be Thy name" (Mt 6:9). God's fatherhood extended to each and to all; this motif recurs throughout the Sermon on the Mount (Mt 5–7), which we can fairly call a compact summary of Jesus' teaching. The Sermon on the Mount is thick with father-child language, and most of it refers to God's relationship with each individual in the crowd of Jesus' listeners.

This multitude, then, shared somehow (we'll examine how more closely later in the book) in Jesus' sonship; they, too, could call God "Father." It's difficult for us to imagine how shocking this was to the religious sensibilities of Jesus' time, and the exhilaration it could bring to its first audience. The apostle John—many decades after his own baptism—recalled the fact that he was a son of God with astonishment. "See what love the Father has given us, that we should be called children of God; and so we are" (1 Jn 3:1).

As children of God, Christians could also look to Jesus as their brother—whether or not they descended from the same tribe, the same trustee family—indeed, whether or not they were descendants of Abraham, Isaac, and Israel.

Revolution Number 3

If the Trinity marked a revolution in religious thought, this doctrine signaled a societal revolution as well. Remember that the trustee family rested as the foundation of Israel's society. Jesus Himself belonged to a trustee family, the nation of Israel, the Tribe of Judah (see Mt 1:1–17). His extended family lived together and made its annual pilgrimages to Jerusalem together. This large family was so numerous and so closely knit that Jesus, at age twelve, could disappear for an entire day without His parents worrying about Him (see Lk 2:41–45); Mary and Joseph assumed that their boy was somewhere safe in the family's large caravan, "among their kinsfolk and acquaintances." All of these kinsfolk could claim, by law and by custom, to be Jesus' "brothers and sisters." The language Jesus spoke made no distinction between siblings and cousins; all were equally brothers and sisters. And that family bond was ethnic, local, and exclusive. One's first duty was to the clan, the trustee family.

Yet Jesus' idea of brotherhood—based on God's fatherhood—seemed to subvert this tribal notion, subordinating the natural family to a new, *supernatural* family established by His New Covenant. Consider this scene: "And His mother and His brothers came; and standing outside they sent to Him and called Him. And a crowd was sitting about Him; and they said to Him, 'Your mother and Your brothers are outside, asking for You.' And He replied, 'Who are My mother and My brothers?' And looking around on those who sat about Him, He said, 'Here are My mother and My brothers! Whoever does the will of God is My brother, and sister, and mother'" (Mk 3:31–35).

In that crowd stood many who were outside Jesus' tribe; yet Jesus clearly saw them as His closest kin, so close that they enjoyed the same status as His blood relatives, including His mother.

This new conception must have seemed subversive. Jesus acknowledged as much and even indicated that the old tribal families could not accommodate the new arrangement He had come to reveal. To live as a child of God, one would first have to distance oneself from tribal exclusivity and insularity. "If any one comes to Me and does not hate his own father and mother and wife and children and brothers and sisters, yes, and even his own life, he cannot be My disciple" (Lk 14:26).

Still, in becoming a disciple, in doing the will of God, the Christian gained a greater family. Jesus said, "Truly, I say to you, there is no one who has left house or brothers or sisters or mother or father or children or lands, for My sake and for the Gospel, who will not receive a hundredfold now in this time, houses and brothers and sisters and mothers and children and lands" (Mk 10:29–30). *Brothers, sisters, mothers, children, houses,* and *lands*—together, those things defined the boundaries of the trustee family, the tribe.

Yes, Jesus was calling His listeners beyond that arrangement; but He was calling them to something that was clearly analogous to the tribal society. In describing the rewards of discipleship, He used the traditional family vocabulary; He described the very trappings of the trustee family.

Beyond Ethnicity

According to Jesus, God was not merely the "God of our fathers." He was the universal Father, and God's family transcended all national, tribal, and familial divisions.

Sociologist Rodney Stark has remarked on the stunning novelty of this Christian achievement: "a religion free of ethnicity."

Moreover, it was a religion free of class distinctions. Take up and read one of the most neglected books of the Bible, St. Paul's Letter to Philemon. In hardly more than a page, the apostle shows how the bond of Christians in Christ has radically reconfigured their social relations. Paul writes in order to reconcile Onesimus, a runaway slave, with his master, Philemon. Paul urges Philemon to take Onesimus back, "no longer as a slave but more than a slave, as a beloved brother, especially to me but how much more to you, both in the flesh and in the Lord" (Phil 16). Elsewhere, Paul spells out the new equality of everyone in the family of God: "For in Christ Jesus you are all sons of God, through faith. . . . There is neither Jew nor Greek, there is neither slave nor free, there is neither male nor female; for you are all one in Christ Jesus" (Gal 3:26, 28).

Here again we face an idea that has become shopworn with the centuries. Like the fatherhood of God, the universal brotherhood of man rolls off the tongue easily today, but most people mean it in a sentimental way, without a hint of the supernatural. The fatherhood of God and the brotherhood of man—one statement seems to require the other. Even apart from any explicit religious context, the human family remains, in today's world, an article of secular faith. Organizations such as the United Nations operate on the assumption that all citizens of all nations share a common humanity, with common rights and common duties.

This very idea, however, the modern world owes to the patrimony of Christendom. To tribal societies, the notion of universality—especially in religious matters— was nonsense. "The people" and "the people of God" were terms synonymous with *"my* people."

Into this milieu, Christianity arrived, offering, according to Rodney Stark, "a new idea." "Among the pagans, you get the sense that no one took care of anyone else except in the tribal way. . . . You take care of your brothers, and you kill everybody else. Christianity told the Greco-Roman world that the definition of 'brother' has got to be a lot broader. There are some things you owe to any living human being."

What a remarkable turn of events. In Genesis, we saw that it was *not good* for man to be alone—that God made us to draw together in families. Yet, in the Gospel, we learn further that God Himself became a man in order to draw men and women *away from* their primal families, their tribes, and toward . . . what?

Since Jesus used family language to describe this new arrangement, we can only speak of it as a family. Indeed, He described our initiation as being "born anew" (Jn 3:3). He spoke of our bond with God as a "new covenant" (Lk 22:20). He spoke of our ultimate destiny as a "marriage supper" (Rv 19:9). Birth, covenant, and marriage have one thing in common: They incorporate an individual into a natural family.

Yet apparently no natural family—not even the much-extended trustee family—could fulfill humanity's deepest desires. The problem with the ancient tribes was not that they were too big and unwieldy, but that they were too small to suffice.

God gave us life in a natural family to lead us to a greater life, a larger family, a supernatural family: a family as big as God.

CHAPTER 4

THE GOD WHO IS FAMILY

W HERE CAN WE find a family to fulfill our needs? How can we find the love for which God made us? God suggested the answer in the story of our creation, and He revealed the way home in the Gospel of Jesus Christ.

Let's return to the beginning, then, to the Book of Genesis, this time to search out the first hints of our ultimate family identity.

Through five and a half days, God called creation into being with the words "Let there be," followed by the name of the thing to be created: light, firmament, waters, stars, fish, birds, and beasts. Midway through the sixth day, however, He suddenly changed His pattern of speaking. "Then God said, 'Let Us make man in Our image, after Our likeness; and let them have dominion' over all creation" (Gn 1:26).

Look closely at that line, and you'll notice a significant

shift in God's language. For the creation of all the rest of the world, He had merely issued His fiat. But when the time came to make man, God—Who is indivisibly one—began to refer to Himself in the first-person plural: "Let *Us* make man in *Our* image, after *Our* likeness." What in heaven could He have meant by this?

What's more, He made it clear that "man," too, is a plurality. "Let Us make *man* in Our image, after Our likeness; and let *them* have dominion." In the next verse, the author of Genesis elaborates: "So God created *man* in His own image, in the image of God He created *him;* male and female He created *them*" (1:27).

Through the first five and a half days described in Genesis, God created a world that would glorify Him and bear His mark. For all of nature tells of God, as every work of art reveals something about the artist. Yet on the sixth day, God formed the first creature that would bear the very image and likeness of the invisible God. Moreover, He made that creature to be a unity only in plurality—and God spoke of Himself in the plural to issue that command.

God Is One, but Not Solitary

This peculiar language—*we* and *us*—appears elsewhere in the Old Testament: Gn 3:22 and 11:7, for example. Some scholars dismiss the usage as a residue of primitive, pre-Israelite worship of many gods. Others say it is merely the author's projection of the "royal we"—the first-person plural used by kings and queens when they speak for themselves and their people, or themselves and God.

I find neither explanation satisfactory. Genesis stands as a carefully crafted literary and theological work. It is unlikely that an author of such prodigy could simply miss several rather blatant instance of leftover paganism. Moreover, though Genesis passed through many manuscript editions and condensations down through the ages, none of its ancient editors chose to tamper with those plural pronouns.

The "royal we" hypothesis, while tenable on one level, still points us to a deeper truth—what Pope John Paul II called the "divine We." For God here could not be speaking for anyone else. "Let Us make man in Our image, after Our likeness." "Us" here can only mean God, and it must mean God alone.

Yet can we accurately describe such a God as "alone"? The answer to that question lies hidden in the plural pronouns of the Book of Genesis, but fully revealed with the Gospel of Jesus Christ. Only in the Gospel can we see clearly why the human creature must be a family before it can fully be God's image. Jesus speaks of His Father as a distinct person, someone to Whom Jesus prays, someone to Whom Jesus goes. Yet

Jesus and the Father are also a unity. Jesus also speaks of another divine Person, the Counselor (Jn 15:26), the Holy Spirit (Jn 20:22), Who will come to the disciples after Jesus has ascended to heaven.

At the end of Matthew's Gospel, as Jesus prepares to ascend to heaven, He reveals the name of God to His disciples. This would arrive as another startling revelation. Till that time, the Israelites considered God's "name"—His innermost identity—ineffable, unutterable. Yet Jesus speaks it as something intimate, a family name: "the name of the Father and of the Son and of the Holy Spirit" (Mt 28:19).

No one thought to correct Our Lord, pointing out that there seem to be *three* names in His statement, though He used the singular word "name." In this line, as in that first chapter of Genesis, there appears to be a paradox: a plurality yet a unity. The *Catechism of the Catholic Church* presents this straightforwardly, explaining that we speak of the "name" and not the "names," because "there is only one God, the almighty Father, His only Son, and the Holy Spirit: the Most Holy Trinity" (no. 233).

God, then, is three; yet God is one. This is the mystery of the Trinity, "the central mystery of Christian faith and life . . . the mystery of God in Himself . . . the source of all the other mysteries of faith, the light that enlightens them" (CCC, no. 234).

It was not good for man to be alone, because alone he

could not fulfill his purpose in creation. God is not solitary, so man could not be solitary. Alone, he could not bear the image and likeness of God.

God's Family Properties

Again, when God revealed His name, He revealed Himself fully—and He revealed Himself as family: as Father, Son, and Holy Spirit. Of this awesome revelation, Pope John Paul II wrote, "In the light of the New Testament it is possible to discern how the primordial model of the family is to be sought in God Himself, in the Trinitarian mystery of His life. The divine 'We' is the eternal pattern of the human 'we,' especially of that 'we' formed by the man and the woman created in the divine image and likeness."

Elsewhere, the same Pope stated, "God in His deepest mystery is not a solitude, but a family, since He has in Himself fatherhood, sonship, and the essence of the family, which is love." He proceeded to identify this "love" with the third Person of the Trinity, the Holy Spirit.

Now, we must be very careful readers here, because many people understand these statements precisely backward, which means they don't understand them at all. The Pope was *not* saying that God is *like* a family. He was *not* presenting the family as a cozy, homey metaphor for the Trinity. He said that God *is* a family. Thus, it would be more accurate to say that my wife, my kids, and I are like a family than to say that God is like a family.

God is not *like* a family. He *is* a family. From eternity, God alone possesses the essential attributes of a family, and the Trinity alone possesses them in their perfection. Earthly households have these attributes, but only by analogy and imperfectly.

Of course, Father, Son, and Holy Spirit are not "gender" terms, but relational terms. The language of the divine family is theological, not biological. The terms, rather, describe the eternal relations of the divine Persons Who dwell in communion.

The Trinity from Infinity

Those terms are not arbitrary. God Himself has revealed them, and they most perfectly express Who God eternally is. The Trinity is God's personal identity, which does not depend upon creation. Other titles—such as Architect, Shepherd, and Physician—are metaphorical terms that describe His relationship to creatures in creaturely terms. God is "Architect" only after fashioning the universe. He is "Physician" only when He has imperfect creatures who need healing. He is "Shepherd" only when He has creatures to guide and protect. Yet, *before creation, from all eternity,* He is Father, Son, and Holy Spirit. This is His proper name. Only "Father, Son, and Holy Spirit," the divine name, reveals God's essential identity in terms that do not depend upon creation.

The importance of this language hit me one Sunday

while attending Mass at a small parish in the Midwest. Standing up front, next to the priest, was the director of religious education, a religious sister. She began by making the Sign of the Cross while intoning, "We gather together in the name of the Creator, the Redeemer, and the Sanctifier."

Now, I knew that this language was in vogue—because it was "gender-neutral"—but I had never actually heard anyone using it. It immediately struck me as wrong, quite apart from any consideration of liturgical norms or political agenda. At first I wasn't sure why her words bothered me, but then it suddenly dawned on me: We were no longer naming God in terms of Who God *is,* from eternity. Rather, we were addressing Him simply in terms of what He has *done*—for us, in history. Of course, there's nothing wrong with acknowledging God's works (of creation, redemption, and sanctification); but, the act of *thanksgiving* is a lesser expression of worship than *praise*—which we render precisely for Who God is. And, no matter how old creation may be, it's definitely not eternal, as God is; thus, God cannot be an eternal Creator (much less an eternal Redeemer or Sanctifier).

In short, to draw a family analogy: It's good for us to tell our loved ones how much we appreciate what they do for us; but it's far better to tell them how much we love them for who they are as persons. They are lovable not because of what we get out of them, but because they are who they are. No one wants to feel used. We should look upon persons, then, not as mere means to our pleasure and advantage, but as ends in themselves. This is still more true of the God Who is three Persons.

The Terrestrial Trinity

No earthly family has so closely resembled the Blessed Trinity as the family of Jesus Himself. Indeed, it is tremendously significant that God Himself chose to be born into a human family. He could have entered history in any number of different ways; He is almighty. His conception, after all, took place without a human father's physical cooperation. Nothing could have stopped God from becoming a man without a mother as well, if that had been His will.

But that was not His will; nor was it fitting. In the words of Pope John Paul II: "The only-begotten Son . . . entered into human history through the family." In this way, Christ could teach us, by example, the deepest truths about the family, the Church, and the Trinity. John Paul continues: "The divine mystery of the Incarnation of the Word thus has an intimate connection with the human family. Not only with one family, that of Nazareth, but in some way with every family. . . . In this sense, both man and the family constitute the way of the Church."

There is a sense, too, in which God established the household of Mary and Joseph as a new Eden. "Whereas Adam and Eve were the source of evil which was unleashed on the world, Joseph and Mary are the summit from which holiness spreads over all the earth." In Nazareth, the human family got a second chance, a new beginning.

Within His Holy Family, Jesus lived a life that was an earthly image of the eternal Trinity. How fitting that devotional writers and artists have often portrayed the Holy Family as an "earthly trinity," which, again in the words of Pope John Paul II, "so admirably reflects the life of communion and love of the eternal Trinity."

A More Perfect Union

How do we bring all this home? That's the stuff of the rest of this book.

This much we know now: When God made humankind in the divine image and likeness, the Trinity was creating the primordial image of Itself. Male and female, He created them both. Then His first utterance was "be fruitful and multiply." What can we infer from that? He was not merely making them to "breed" like the animals and reproduce. The man and the woman were to become "one," and the one they became was not a *one* they chose, but a *one* that God had designed. This was more than physical and psychological communion, though it included that as well. The one they became was so real that, nine months later, they had to give it a name. The Church calls the family a "communion of persons" united in love; that's the very same definition it applies to the Trinity.

Thus it remains today. In the family, we become three-in-one, imaging the triune God. Now, that's power. Indeed, no other natural act makes humans more godlike. Marital love best translates this divine language so that human beings can learn to speak it fluently and honestly.

Marriage, then, provides the most perfect image of our ultimate home. Still, it is only an image. Human marriage is a living, embodied analogy that points the way to something greater.

From the beginning, the Trinity is the family we were made for, the home we have desired. How we get there, how we live there, is for another chapter.

CHAPTER 5

THE GOD WHO IS COVENANT

T HE WORLD," SAID the poet Gerard Manley
Hopkins, "is charged with the grandeur of
God."

It's an odd idea, when you think about it. Christians,
after all, do not worship nature; nor do we identify God
with the world. He is infinitely superior to His creation,
infinitely grander than the earth's canyons, waterfalls, rain
forests, and mountain peaks. He transcends all the things
He has made. His true grandeur, then, is invisible to the
eye. "No one has ever seen God" (1 Jn 4:12).

Still, Hopkins was right. The world *is* charged with
God's grandeur. St. Bonaventure tells us that "the world
was made for the glory of God"; and he goes on to explain that God created all things "not to increase His
glory, but to show it forth and communicate it" (see
CCC, no. 293). God's transcendence does not leave creation completely without a clue. Creation does tell us
something about its creator. So we can learn more about

Who God is by observing the grandeur of what He does. In everything that exists, we may discern—with the eyes of faith—a familial purpose, what the early Christians called "the footprints of the Trinity" *(vestigia Trinitatis).*

We note that many good things come in threes. Time falls neatly into three dimensions: past, present, and future. We measure area by its height, width, and depth, and light by its particle, wave, and beam. Physicists examine matter according to energy, motion, and phenomena. Nature's seeming preference for threeness inspired one recent theologian to speak of the "triunity of the universe."

In the Scriptures, God Himself has revealed the family as an earthly sign especially charged with the grandeur of the Trinity. "Let Us make man in Our image, after Our likeness. . . . So God created man in His own image, in the image of God He created him; male and female He created them." When a man and woman become one, they beget a third; and the three constitute a unity.

Just as the structure of a crystal is evident in every particle of the crystal, so the mark of the Trinity is the "crystalline" structure in creation, and this is especially evident in the family.

It's the Economy

We discern God most clearly in His revelation of Himself. If He had not revealed Himself as Father, Son, and Holy Spirit, we could not have discerned this truth from mere observation of nature. Indeed, though humanity often discerned God's unity, no philosopher, no theologian, brought all the evidence to a Trinitarian conclusion until Jesus Himself revealed it to be true. For the Trinity is a mystery that surpasses our unaided powers of reason. This does not mean that belief in God is irrational. It means, rather, that any god we could comprehend could not be God, because such a "divinity" would be inferior to our own minds. God's grandeur can be glimpsed, for fleeting moments, in creation. But we cannot *know* God unless He reveals Himself.

Once He has revealed Himself, then matters become clearer. Then we can see how the world tells of His grandeur. Moreover, once we know God as Trinity, we can better understand the mysteries of the world. Reflection on the mystery of God and the mysteries of creation becomes mutually enhancing.

The *Catechism of the Catholic Church* explains how many saints and thinkers have approached the interdependence of our knowledge of God and knowledge of creation.

> *The Fathers of the Church distinguish between theology* (theologia) *and economy* (oikonomia). *"Theology" refers to the mystery of God's inmost life within the Blessed Trinity and "economy" to all the works by which God reveals Himself and communicates His life. Through the* oikonomia *the* theologia *is revealed to us; but con-*

versely, the theologia *illuminates the whole* oikonomia.
God's works reveal Who He is in Himself; the mystery
of His inmost being enlightens our understanding of all
His works. So it is, analogously, among human persons.
A person discloses himself in his actions, and the better we
know a person, the better we understand his actions.
(CCC, no. 236)

It is interesting to note that even the word "economy"
has a familial meaning. It comes from the Greek words
oikos ("home") and *nomos* ("law"). Creation's economy is
the law of God's household. It is how He fathers His
family throughout salvation history.

Chief among God's works in this "economy" is His
revelation. God's definitive self-revelation to the world is
His Son, Jesus Christ, sent "in the fullness of time" (Gal
4:4). Yet, as we have seen, He has left us clues all along,
from the first moment of creation, building them into
human nature. From age to age, He has gathered a people to Himself. The story of His people unfolds in the
Bible.

Seventh Heaven

The Bible begins with the story we keep coming back to
in this book: the story of creation. God made Adam not
as yet another one of the animals, but in the divine image and likeness. These terms speak volumes about man's

original status in God's sight. The same words appear next in Gn 5:3, when the Bible tells us that Adam fathered a son named Seth, "in his own likeness, after his image."

Made in Adam's image and likeness, Seth was truly Adam's son, and Adam was truly Seth's father. Made in God's image and likeness, then, Adam was truly . . . God's son! And God was truly his Father.

How could this be? Though God is Father from all eternity, His fatherhood does not depend on human beings. Moreover, humans—though made in God's image—are still not the same sort of being as God. So how could Adam enter into a *family* relationship with God, Who is almighty, infinite, and eternal?

The answer lies in the details of Adam's creation. God made him on the sixth day, but for the sake of the seventh day. It is the seventh day, the sabbath, that God "blessed" and "hallowed" and declared a day of rest (Gn 2:2–3). Now, why would God do this? He is almighty, so He does not grow tired; He had no need of a sabbath snooze. What purpose, then, could the sabbath serve?

Let's look more closely. The sabbath is the seventh day, and the Hebrew word for "seven" is *sheba*. Yet *sheba* stands not only for a number. *Sheba* is also a verb, and it means to swear a covenant oath—literally, to "seven oneself" (see, for example, Abraham's covenant oath in Gn 21:27–32). The number seven is the unmistakable sign of a covenant.

The sabbath, then, stood as a sign of God's covenant with creation (see Ex 31:16–17). The sabbath symbolized man's God-given destiny: to rest in God's blessing and holiness for all eternity. "The sabbath was made for man," Jesus said (Mk 2:27).

Specifically, the seventh day signified the sealing of the covenant family bond between God and man. Remember, from chapter 2, that ancient families were closely knit and exclusive of outsiders—but that outsiders could be "adopted" into the tribe by means of a covenant. What sealed or renewed the bond was the covenant oath.

With the seventh day, God was making a covenant with mankind. God took Adam and Eve into His family. God made them His children.

With this shift in relationship comes a corresponding shift in language. In the first chapter of Genesis, we read of God as "Elohim," a formal name, usually translated into English simply as "God." Elohim evokes the divine power in the act of creation. In the second chapter, how-ever—immediately in the wake of the seventh day—God appears as "Yahweh Elohim," which is usually translated into English as "the Lord God." This is more than a mere multiplication of honorific titles. "Yahweh"—which, I repeat, appears only after the seventh day—is a personal name, a family name. Something has changed in the re-lationship between God and creation. Most especially, something has changed in the relationship between God and His highest creation, the creature made in His image and likeness, the only creature who can be called God's child.

As a result of the seventh day, the day of the oath, God lives in covenant, a family bond, with humankind (see CCC, no. 288). God is not just our creator but our Father.

The Setting Son

In the Genesis account, Adam receives many of the tasks that ancient readers would recognize as belonging to a family's firstborn son. God commanded Adam to till (in Hebrew, *'abodah)* and to guard (in Hebrew, *shamar)* the garden where he would live (see Gn 2:15). In doing so, God placed Adam not only as a landowner and laborer but also as a priest; for those two words, *'abodah* and *shamar,* appear together elsewhere in the Pentateuch only in reference to the Levites' priestly service in Israel (see Nm 3:7–8; 8:26; 18:5–6).

Till and guard: These were the terms of the covenant. Then "be fruitful and multiply" (Gn 1:28). The Father would raise up His son, Adam, to be a father himself, a father who would in turn raise up many children to God. All Adam had to do was to be faithful to God in these things—and observe one other condition. "And the Lord God commanded the man, saying, 'You may freely eat of every tree of the garden; but of the tree of the knowledge of good and evil you shall not eat, for in the day that you eat of it you shall die'" (Gn 2:16–17).

In hindsight, it seems a small requirement. Adam could live as a son of God, have all his wants satisfied, find all his work rewarding, and never die. He could eat the fruit of any tree but one. If he ate of that tree, death would surely follow.

Yet Adam violated the covenant. He sinned. He ate the fruit of that forbidden tree, and he brought death and suffering upon himself and all his offspring. Worst of all, in breaking the covenant, he separated himself and all his offspring from God's family. (See CCC, nos. 403–4.)

Bound by covenant to live forever as a son of God, Adam chose instead to live outside the family as a slave. (We'll come back to this story a little later and examine it in greater detail.)

Widening Family Circles

In sinning, Adam and Eve turned their back on God and chose to be banished from their homeland. God, however, did not abandon them or their children. Again and again, He "offered a covenant to man, and through the prophets taught him to hope for salvation" (Eucharistic Prayer IV). Indeed, immediately after Adam and Eve sinned, God promised them that one of their descendants would vanquish the serpent and restore the inheritance that the first parents had lost (see Gn 3:15).

In the Old Testament, we read of God renewing His covenant on four more occasions: to Noah, to Abraham, to Moses, and to David. With each succeeding covenant, God opened membership in His covenant family to ever more people: first to a married couple, then to a household, then to a tribe, then to a nation, then to a kingdom. When God preserved the family of Noah, he swore never again to destroy the earth by flood (see Gn 9:8–17). The sign of the covenant with Noah was the rainbow. When God led Abraham to the Promised Land, He pledged that Abraham's tribe would increase and bring blessing to all the earth (see Gn 12:1–3; 22:16–18). The sign of the covenant with Abraham was circumcision. When God worked through Moses to lead Israel out of Egypt and into Canaan, He promised to make the Israelites a holy nation of priests, restoring the inheritance of Abraham and the rights and duties of Adam (see Ex 19:5–6). The sign of the covenant with Moses was the Passover. Then, to David, God promised to build a worldwide kingdom and restore all people to proper worship (see 2 Sm 7:8–19). The sign of this covenant was the dynastic throne of the House of David.

Economic Shortfalls

All of this brings us back to the relationship between theology and economy—Who God is and what He does. We learn about God from the things we see Him do. We learn about creation by examining it in light of what we know of God.

Through covenants, God formed and re-formed His human family. Through covenants, He made and remade our earthly families in His own familial image and likeness. Covenant is the bond that holds a family together. Covenant is *what God does,* because covenant is *Who God is.* We read in the New Testament that "God is love" (1 Jn 4:16), a statement one can make only of a God Who is family—a God Who lives in an eternal communion of three Persons, a God Who lives eternally in covenant.

We, for our part, have repeatedly fallen short of that eternal covenant. Each of the Old Testament covenants failed in its turn. Every time God sought to restore humanity's family bond with the creator, humans chose again to sin and break the bond. God remained constantly faithful; Adam did not, and neither did Noah, neither did Moses, neither did David.

In fact, sacred history leads us to conclude that *only God* keeps His covenant promises. How, then, could humans fulfill their end of a covenant in a way that would last forever? That would require a person to be as sinless and as constant as God Himself.

CHAPTER 6

THE GOD WHO IS LOVE

I T'S FAIR TO ask, at this point, if people are just plain crazy.

Sin seems irrational beyond explanation. Adam had everything in the world. He was married to the woman created especially for him. God had given him dominion over the entire earth, with all its real estate, livestock, and produce. His natural gifts were so impressive that even God had declared them "very good." What's more, God had endowed both Adam and Eve with gifts over and above their nature—the "preternatural" gifts. Among these, they enjoyed an intelligence endowed with super-human power. They were immortal, too; though material bodies are, by nature, subject to decay and death, God had given the primal couple immunity from dying.

Yet all this is nothing compared to God's crowning gift: "Then the Lord God formed man of dust from the ground, and breathed into his nostrils the breath of life; and man became a living being" (Gn 2:7). God did not merely activate man; He *animated* him with His own breath, His own Spirit. Thus, we see that Adam was supernaturally graced with divine sonship even as he drew his first breath. His first glimpse of creation was illuminated by the Holy Spirit.

Adam had the most impressive array of natural, preternatural, and supernatural qualities. Yet he forfeited it all and chose death for himself and for his earthly family. This seems insane. What happened?

Making Sense of the Story

Many people try to explain Adam's disobedience in terms of pure malice—a declaration of war against God. Adam, however, was not an evil man. God Himself had given Adam the Holy Spirit and pronounced His creation "good." Moreover, even if Adam had been consumed with self-interest, obedience should have won out. The serpent could offer Adam nothing by way of a bribe, for in Eden Adam lacked nothing.

Others see Adam as naïve in his innocence of evil, and so an easy dupe for the wily serpent. But this, too, seems implausible to me. Here was a man with preternatural intelligence. He could look at the animals, know them, and name them. He should not have been seduced or hoodwinked by a wild creature.

I believe there's more to the story than that. Let's look closely at the temptation passage in Genesis, to try to walk a mile in Adam's bare feet—to try and truly understand God's command, the serpent's counteroffer, and Adam's fatal motivation.

Garden Duty

Before we can understand Adam's sin, we must try to hear God's commandment as Adam would have heard it:

> *And the Lord God planted a garden in Eden, in the east; and there He put the man whom He had formed. And out of the ground the Lord God made to grow every tree that is pleasant to the sight and good for food, the tree of life also in the midst of the garden, and the tree of the knowledge of good and evil. . . . The Lord God took the man and put him in the garden of Eden to till it and keep it. And the Lord God commanded the man, saying, "You may freely eat of every tree of the garden; but of the tree of the knowledge of good and evil you shall not eat, for in the day that you eat of it you shall die." (Gn 2:8–9, 15–17)*

There are many oddities in this passage. They are not so odd for us, perhaps, living as we are in a world of darkness and shadows, but they certainly should seem odd to a man living in a perfect world.

In the preceding chapter, we discussed God's command to till and keep the garden. To till the garden seems reasonable enough. But remember that the Hebrew word translated as "to keep" means, literally, "to guard," as the Israelite priests guarded the sanctuary and kept it from defilement. Why should Adam have to guard paradise? God's command implied that there was something that must be kept *out,* something that might try to get in.

A second oddity appears in God's threat of punishment: "in the day that you eat of it you shall die." In some translations, the last phrase appears as "you shall most surely die." The Hebrew idiom is difficult to render in English. Translated verbatim, the text reads: "you shall die die" or "you shall die the death." It's a strange construction, the repetition of the word "die" or "death." The Hebrew language uses repetition—as English uses the *-est* suffix in, for example, "greatest" or "weakest"—to indicate a superlative. (When God says that He found creation "very good," the Hebrew actually reads "good good.") The words "die" and "death," however, rarely appear in the superlative. After all, Adam couldn't get any deader than dead, could he?

Well, maybe he could. The ancient rabbis taught that this passage of Genesis implied that there are two kinds of death. "The death of the man is the separation of the soul from the body," wrote Philo of Alexandria, a Jewish contemporary of Jesus. "But the death of the soul is the decay of virtue and the bringing in of wickedness. It is for this reason that God says not only 'die' but 'die the death,' indicating not the death common to us all, but that special death, which is that of the soul becoming entombed in passions and wickedness of all kinds. And this death is practically the antithesis of the death which awaits us all."

The terms seem very clear now and even absurdly simple. If Adam kept God's one small commandment, he would live his blissful life forever. If he didn't, he would die the most extreme sort of death. It's fair, though, for us to ask whether Adam could have understood the consequences of sin. What could death mean to a man who was preternaturally immune to death? For that matter, why did God plant the tree of life in the garden? Could such threats and such elixirs hold any meaning to an immortal man?

Yes, they could, and they did. Though God had made man preternaturally immortal, He had also made Adam's body, which was mortal by nature, with a healthy, instinctive abhorrence of physical death. Otherwise, His threatened punishment—"the day that you eat of it you shall die"—would make no sense.

Trouble in Paradise

Now that we've examined the terms of God's command, let's give the serpent his due, looking over the fine print of his proposition:

> *Now the serpent was more subtle than any other wild creature that the Lord God had made. He said to the woman, "Did God say, 'You shall not eat of any tree of*

the garden'?" And the woman said to the serpent, "We may eat of the fruit of the trees of the garden; but God said, 'You shall not eat of the fruit of the tree which is in the midst of the garden, neither shall you touch it, lest you die.' " But the serpent said to the woman, "You will not die. For God knows that when you eat of it your eyes will be opened, and you will be like God, knowing good and evil." So when the woman saw that the tree was good for food, and that it was a delight to the eyes, and that the tree was to be desired to make one wise, she took of its fruit and ate; and she also gave some to her husband, and he ate. Then the eyes of both were opened, and they knew that they were naked; and they sewed fig leaves together and made themselves aprons. (Gn 3:1–7)

Once again, in the original Hebrew we encounter many curious details that get lost in the translation. First, we may note that the serpent addresses not just Eve but Adam as well. He uses second-person-plural verbs, a construction we lack in English (except in Southern dialects in the United States, which use "y'all" for the plural form). For most English speakers, the word "you" means the *person or persons* who are being addressed. But Hebrew, like most other languages, makes a distinction between singular *you* and plural *you.*

The serpent speaks not to one person, but to the couple—yet who responds? Only Eve.

Where, then, is the man whom God commanded to

guard the garden? He's there. The serpent addresses him, but Adam is silent. He allows his wife to take up the serpent's challenge; he allows her to continue the discussion . . . and he allows her to succumb to the serpent's proposal. Why?

Silence Not Golden

To understand this, we have to return again to the beginning of the narrative, to the time when God made Adam. Adam lived then in the presence of God as a son of God. Yet this aloneness was not good. God created Eve to be Adam's companion and to make the divine image more perfect in humankind. But I believe that, even then, the work of man's creation was not complete. God left something of the divine image *for man and woman to bring to completion.* God wanted man and woman in the human family, to imitate the communion, the covenant, that is at the heart of the divine family, the Trinity.

This is why God permitted Adam and Eve to undergo the ordeal with the serpent—which was surely an imposing and deadly beast. Elsewhere in the Old Testament, the Hebrew word here translated as "serpent," *nahash,* denotes a dragon (see Is 27:1) or a sea monster (Jb 26:13).

What is clear is that Adam faced a life-threatening force, deadly in its intent and formidable in its subtlety. Moreover, the serpent seized on the one thing that humans had been created to dread instinctively: dying. The *Catechism of the Catholic Church* identifies the serpent as Satan (see no. 391) and spells out the power he had to seduce Adam, but also to harm him physically and spiritually (nos. 395 and 394).

All these circumstances pack power into the serpent's words. In contradicting God's command, the serpent said, "You will not die." Quoting the Lord God only partially, the serpent dropped the second "die," omitting the superlative. In doing so, he subtly shifted the subject of conversation from one type of death to another, from spiritual death ("die die") to physical death.

Moreover, the serpent uttered an incomplete statement, leaving his thought unfinished, and leaving Adam and Eve to fill in the blank. "You will not die . . . ," the serpent said. The couple would not die, he implied, *if they ate the fruit*. The flip side, then, can be read as a threat: They *would* die if they *refused* to eat the fruit. They would die physically, and he would make sure of it.

Now, if the serpent was indeed a monstrous beast, and if Adam did indeed dread death, then suddenly we can understand our forefather's silence. *He feared his own death*. Moreover, he feared his physical death more than he feared offending God by sin. He stood by quietly while Eve continued in conversation with the beast. He stood in silence while the serpent issued his veiled threat. The serpent addressed Adam, but the man never responded. Nor did he call out to God for help. In pride and in fear, he kept silent. And, with his wife, he disobeyed the command of the Lord.

What we have here is far more than a failure of nerve or breakdown in communications. It's a failure of faith, hope, and love. Adam's fears kept him from his duty to guard the garden. They kept him from trusting in his Father God, and they threw him back, in pride, upon himself. They kept him even from defending his wife—the flesh of his flesh, bone of his bone.

Knowing the serpent's power, Adam was unwilling to lay down his own life—for the sake of his love of God, or to save the life of his beloved. That refusal to sacrifice was Adam's original sin. He committed it even before he had tasted the fruit, even before Eve had tasted the fruit.

Trial by Fear

The serpent had achieved his aim. He had deceived the couple, but subtly, never lying outright. Indeed, the narrative seems to prove him right at every turn. God had told Adam that on the very day he ate the fruit, he would surely die. The serpent, for his part, said, "You will not die." And Adam and Eve didn't "die" on that day—at least not in the way the serpent meant the verb "die." The serpent also promised the couple, "your eyes will be opened, and you will be like God, knowing good and evil" (Gn 3:5); and, sure enough, two verses later we read, "Then the eyes of both were opened." And as if to fulfill every last word of the serpent's prediction, the chapter ends with the Lord God saying, "Behold, the man has become like one of Us, knowing good and evil" (3:22).

It appears that the serpent got it right on every count. Adam and Eve didn't die; their eyes were opened; and they became "like" God, knowing good and evil. The serpent was right because he kept his conversation to the natural order. What he knew, but did not say, was that there was a greater, supernatural order.

For the tree was good. Eve saw that (Gn 3:6). It was a natural good. It looked good, and it could do good—giving wisdom to the person who ate it. But God had commanded the first couple to sacrifice this great good for the sake of a higher good—a supernatural good.

Just as there is life that is natural and life that is supernatural, there is death that is natural and death that is supernatural. In choosing a natural good, Eve and Adam rejected the supernatural good: divine sonship. In choosing to save their natural life—the only thing the devil really had the power to take—Adam and Eve chose to die spiritually.

Adam and Eve had no natural sense of supernatural life, so they had no natural abhorrence of supernatural death. They did sense their natural life—their breath, thoughts, consciousness—and so they had a natural and wholesome abhorrence of natural death. Indeed, they possessed a natural wisdom to preserve life and avoid death.

But before they could choose supernatural life and

avoid supernatural death, they needed supernatural wisdom. Only then could they have recognized supernatural death as being even more deadly than bodily death.

The only way they could protect supernatural life would be to take a step into the darkness of faith. God had placed them in a situation where supernatural faith was the *only* reason to obey in the face of bodily harm. Supernatural hope would have enabled them to endure hardship. And ultimately, supernatural love would have led them to fear offending God more than they feared the loss of natural life and preternatural gifts. Faith, hope, and love would have been perfected in that moment if they had called on the name of the Lord. But, instead, "Man, tempted by the devil, let his trust in his Creator die in his heart" (CCC, no. 397).

What Adam and Eve needed was not complete fearlessness, but rather a better sort of fear. For there is a good sort of fear, a holy fear, and it's called the fear of the Lord. "The fear of the Lord is the beginning of wisdom" (Ps 111:10). "The fear of the Lord is the crown of wisdom" (Sir 1:18). Such fear is supernatural awe, leading to supernatural wisdom. But, for Adam, pride, in the form of a disordered self-reliance, activated the wrong fear: the fear of natural suffering and death. As a result, he ate from the wrong tree.

The right tree, the saving tree, is approachable only by those who enjoy supernatural wisdom because they fear the Lord. For wisdom "is a tree of life to those who lay hold of her" (Prv 3:18).

Like a riddle, the story of Adam and Eve operates on two levels. The drama describes, at once, the natural and supernatural stakes of the first couple's decisions. They had to choose between two kinds of life: natural and supernatural. They had to choose between two kinds of death: physical and spiritual. They had to decide between two kinds of wisdom: human and divine. Ultimately, they faced up to two kinds of fear: the fear of suffering and the fear of the Lord. One would have led them to eat from the tree of life; the other, tragically, led them to eat the forbidden fruit. The riddle would remain unsolved until a New Adam emerged from a garden and approached another tree, a saving tree.

The Inside Story

What was the meaning of this primordial test? How would Adam's self-sacrifice have perfected him as an image of God? God, after all, cannot offer sacrifice. To whom could God possibly offer sacrifice? There is no one greater than He!

Sacrifice, however, is the only way that humans can imitate the interior life of the Trinity. For God is love, and the essence of love is life-giving. The Father pours out the fullness of Himself; He holds nothing of His divinity back. He eternally fathers the Son. The Father is, above all else, a life-giving lover, and the Son is His perfect image. So what else is the Son but a life-giving lover? And the Son dynamically images the Father from all eternity, pouring out the life He's received from the Father; He gives that life back to the Father as a perfect expression of thanks and love. That life and love, which the Son receives from the Father and returns to the Father, *is* the Holy Spirit.

We imitate God by giving ourselves in love. Love demands that we give ourselves totally, holding nothing back. In eternity, the complete gift of self is the Trinity's life. In time, the image of that love is *sacrificial* love, *life-giving* love. We must die to ourselves for the sake of another. This is precisely what Adam failed to do.

And, as a result, he halted his own creation when it was not yet complete. For Adam was made in an earthly paradise, but he was made *for* heavenly life in the Trinity. If he had obeyed God, he would have brought his creation to completion, sharing the very life of God.

Instead, he lost everything. Above all, he lost his divine sonship. It is significant that, when Eve enters into dialogue with the devil, she reverts to calling God "Elohim" rather than the paternal "Yahweh." She was verbally stepping out of her privileged family relation with God and placing herself on a level with the enslaved.

We must not underestimate the dire circumstance of Adam after the Fall—and of all his descendants. A recent theologian summed it up well: "Sin cuts across this one whole process and causes a man to be *monstrously half-created,* to be a Beast. Creation in its fullness includes a moment at which nature dies to itself and rises again, at which the first movement of life flows back upon its source and rises again. So that if one closely studies the creational imagery one finds that it virtually includes the notions of sacrifice, of death, of rebirth or resurrection that go to constitute the terminology of redemption."

By failing to sacrifice his life, Adam left himself and his descendants "monstrously half-created"—until the day when one of those descendants could offer a perfect sacrifice.

Altar Servers

Sacrifice, then, became the essential mark of all subsequent covenants between God and humankind. Noah, at the end of his nautical adventure, "built an altar to the Lord, and took of every clean animal and of every clean bird, and offered burnt offerings on the altar" (Gn 8:20). Noah's sacrifice symbolized everything he possessed, and it marked the moment of God's covenant oath with him.

God's covenant with Abraham followed upon a "test" (Gn 22:1) reminiscent of Adam's. God asked Abraham to sacrifice his only son, Isaac, as a burnt offering upon an altar on Moriah (Gn 22:2). God spared Isaac, and immediately afterward made His covenant promises to Abraham.

The motif continued in the time of Moses, at the

Passover, when God required Israelite families to sacrifice an unblemished lamb in place of their firstborn.

Finally, David's covenant with the Lord reached its consummation in the Jerusalem Temple built by his son, Solomon, where burnt offerings rose daily to the throne of the Almighty.

Every covenant required a sacrifice symbolic of man's total self-giving. For a covenant is not a contract; it is not an exchange of goods. A covenant is an exchange of persons. One person gives up his former self, his former identity, to be accepted into a new family.

Yet every covenant in the Old Testament foundered because of individuals' refusal to give their all. Noah built an ark, but then he got drunk. Abraham acted faithfully in uprooting himself and emigrating to a new land—but then he grew impatient for an heir, and so he took a concubine, a mistress. Moses trusted the Lord, and yet he struck the rock in anger and gave in to his temper. David was a man after God's own heart, yet he committed adultery with Bathsheba. All of these men displayed both tremendous virtue and fatal vice. Look again at Adam himself. We tend to dwell on his failures, but there was much more to his life. He was a father to many children, among them Cain, Abel, and Seth. Yes, he raised the first fratricidal murderer, but he also raised the first martyr.

In each of these chosen men, we find partial fulfillment pointing toward an even greater and more perfect fulfillment. Each of them faced an incredibly challenging task and performed it with faithfulness, and yet failed at a decisive point, showing us that some greater intermediary would have to establish some greater covenant. For nothing less than total self-giving would do. Nothing else could serve to imitate the Trinitarian life.

Sealed with a Curse

Weakened by Adam's sin, no one could give himself completely in imitation of God. Thus, humankind and individual men and women could not enjoy the peace of Trinitarian life or the happiness that only God knows. For faithfulness to the covenant is a precondition of happiness and peace. When we fail in this, we bring misery upon ourselves—not because God is vindictive and bent upon crushing the rebellious, but because happiness is incompatible with any degree of selfishness. When we hold back anything from our self-giving, we choose our own death (see Acts 5:1–11).

This is the option that humans chose repeatedly in the Old Testament, with dire consequences: slavery, captivity, war, exile, family ruin. These were all outward manifestations of an inner human condition: Humanity had lost its inheritance, its divine sonship, its membership in God's Family. And so it had brought upon itself the covenant curses, which are the flip side of the covenant promises.

In His covenants, God promised a greater restoration: a trustee family of countless descendants, a bountiful land, and prosperous and tranquil rule over all the earth. Yet even the greatest men and women of the ancient world could not hold up their end of the oath. Instead, they succumbed to Adam's failure of nerve; they committed Adam's sin and refused to sacrifice *everything* for the sake of love. Thus, they refused love. Flouting the covenant, they refused to allow their human family to complete the image and likeness of the divine family.

What Adam could have preserved by accepting martyrdom, mankind could now win back only by fits and starts, and never in its fullness. To become children of God once again—this was always out of reach.

The First Go'el

God, however, never ceased to be a Father. We see His paternal care in each of the covenants. He always accommodated Himself to His children's condition. Sometimes He did this by speaking as if He were human, with human passions such as anger and regret (witness His "bargaining" with Abraham and Moses in Gn 18 and Ex 33). An earthly father acts similarly with his own children when he stoops to their level or speaks to them in baby talk. At other times, God raised His children up above the mundane, to see divine things, as when He sent His angels to Abraham and Jacob or when He gave the law to Moses. Again, this is a trait we see in human fathers as well, when they give their children grown-up responsibilities in the household. This is the way of God's revelation in history: Sometimes He stoops to our level to speak with us; sometimes He raises us up to live as He lives.

Because of the covenants, the tribes of Israel, for their part, continued to speak of themselves as ʿam Yahweh, "the kin of God." Their tribal kinship, however, was more concrete in their experience, and it was from their earthly family that they expected a "redeeming kinsman" to come and restore their lost fortunes. For with each spiritual infidelity inevitably came material ruin.

The redeeming kinsman—the go'el, or next of kin— was traditionally the hero who avenged a family and its honor. In later times, Israel would speak of this go'el as the Messiah—the "Christ," or "Anointed One"—the one Yahweh would raise up to deliver His kin, redeem them, avenge them, and purify them by offering a pure sacrifice.

Yet even their wildest hopes and dreams could not have prepared them for what was to come.

CHAPTER 7

THE GOD WHO
BECAME MAN

ADAM HAD GIVEN himself over to the power of the serpent. Forfeiting divine sonship, he had chosen death for himself and his progeny. No one could reverse this course of events. "Truly no man can ransom himself," said the Psalmist, "or give to God the price of his life, for the ransom of his life is costly, and can never suffice, that he should continue to live on for ever, and never see the Pit" (Ps 49:7–9).

Just Love

The price for securing divine glory was set "in the beginning," and it was no less than total, life-giving love. Yet no one alive since Adam could volunteer a sinless life, much less afford the price for sharing God's glory. No one could make the offering that Adam, in his time, had failed to make.

Who, then, could imitate the life of God? It would

have to be done by God Himself. Abraham had spoken prophetically as he traveled with Isaac to the place of sacrifice: "God will provide Himself the lamb for a burnt offering" (Gn 22:8).

Thus, God entered history as the "New Adam" (see 1 Cor 15:20–23, 45). The Word, the second Person of the Blessed Trinity, took on flesh and dwelt among God's people (see Jn 1:1–5, 14). This is the mystery of the Incarnation. God Himself would become a man and face the same trials as Adam. Only now, this New Man would prevail over death and sin. Man, in Jesus Christ, would offer himself completely to God in life-giving love, in sacrifice. In space and time, Jesus Christ would carry out the eternal and transcendent love of the Trinity.

By Jesus' own account, this total self-giving was the essence of His mission: "For the Son of man also came not to be served but to serve, and to give His life as a ransom for many" (Mk 10:45).

"I am the good shepherd . . . I lay down My life for the sheep. . . . For this reason the Father loves Me, because I lay down My life. . . . I lay it down of My own accord. I have power to lay it down, and I have power to take it again; this charge I have received from My Father" (Jn 10:14–15, 17–18).

"Truly, truly, I say to you, unless a grain of wheat falls into the earth and dies, it remains alone; but if it dies, it bears much fruit. He who loves his life loses it, and he who hates his life in this world will keep it for eternal life" (Jn 12:24–25).

"Greater love has no man than this, that a man lay down his life for his friends" (Jn 15:13).

The Cross Is a Trinitarian Event

At last had come a Man Who could achieve what Adam would not—a Man Who could keep an everlasting covenant with God, a family bond that no one could break. At last, a Man could give to God the price of His life, and of all human life. At last, Someone could restore the human family and raise it up to the dignity for which it was created, in the beginning. For Jesus was tempted—once again, in a garden (see Jn 18:1)—with the same natural dread of death that Adam faced, but He faced it down. Indeed, it was by the very act of overcoming that natural dread that He won for us a supernatural life. "He Himself likewise partook of the same [human] nature, that through death He might destroy him who has the power of death, and deliver all those who *through fear of death were subject to lifelong bondage*" (Heb 2:14). Being subject to perpetual bondage through Adam's fear of death is the lot we inherited from Adam.

But Christ knew a higher fear than the dread of bodily suffering: He knew the fear of the Lord. And while Adam's pride kept him from calling for help, Christ cried out immediately to the Father. Three times in the Garden of Gethsemane Our Lord fell on His face to plead with the Father (Mt 26:39–44), because, unlike Adam, He feared offending God more than He feared His own death. "In the days of His flesh, Jesus offered up prayers and supplications, with loud cries and tears, to Him Who was able to save Him from death, and He was heard for His godly fear. Although He was a Son, He learned obedience through what He suffered; and being made perfect He became the source of eternal salvation to all who obey Him" (Heb 5:7–9).

Jesus Christ accomplished our salvation by giving Himself, in love, to be crucified. "You were ransomed from the futile ways inherited from your fathers, not with perishable things such as silver or gold, but with the precious blood of Christ" (1 Pt 1:18–19). Instead of losing His life at death, Jesus gave His life. As a result, on Good Friday, death died more than Jesus.

Love is what endowed Christ's suffering and death with its infinite value and power. Opponents of Christianity sometimes claim that other people have suffered more than Jesus. Yet no one has ever loved more. And nowhere is Jesus' love more active than in His obedience unto death.

The Price Is Rite

The price of our redemption was not primarily Christ's pain and suffering, but His life-giving love. It was not so much that Jesus died *in our place* as *for our sake.* Indeed, Christ's passion didn't exempt us from suffering and death; rather, He unites us to Himself and endows our suffering and death with redemptive value and power. St. Paul knew this well: "Now I rejoice in my sufferings for your sake, and in my flesh I complete what is lacking in Christ's afflictions for the sake of His body, that is, the Church" (Col 1:24). The price of our redemption was Christ's perfect love and blameless life given completely, for the sake of another, even unto death.

To understand this is to grasp the true and familial meaning of our salvation. To misunderstand it leads sometimes to unbearable conclusions. Often, people think that Jesus' suffering somehow vented the wrath of a vengeful deity— as if God were an unforgiving judge who needed to exact his pound of flesh from an innocent but willing victim. Such images fall far short of the Gospel truth. For God's love is just, and His justice is loving. "Love is the fulfilling of the law," said St. Paul (Rom 13:10). If, however, we imagine God as an enraged, myopic judge, then we deny both His merciful love and His perfect justice—and we grossly misrepresent the inner logic of His covenant law. For the covenant requires life-giving love as a prerequisite for entrance into the glorious life of the triune family.

Jesus' life, death, and resurrection were a revelation *in time* of the eternal inner life of the Blessed Trinity. The Son returned the Father's gift of love, which was His very life. Nothing less than godlike love would fulfill the covenant.

Through baptism, we share in the sacrificial death of Jesus (see Rom 6:3). The immersion in water symbolizes

His—and our—descent into the tomb. "You were buried with Him in baptism, in which you were also raised with Him through faith in the working of God, Who raised Him from the dead" (Col 2:12). And what is the new life to which we are raised? It is no less than the life of the Trinity. In Christ, we receive what Pope John Paul II called "our sublime vocation as sons in the Son." Christian life, then, is a participation in the life of the Trinity. By God's own life, we are empowered to live and love in a godlike manner. The early Christians dared to call this process *deification,* because they believed in God's capacity to divinize us.

Just one generation away from the time of the apostles, St. Irenaeus wrote, "It was for this end that the Word of God was made man, and He who was the Son of God became the Son of man, that man, having been taken into the Word, and receiving the adoption, might become the son of God." In A.D. 318, St. Athanasius put it most succinctly: "He became man so that we might be made God; and He manifested Himself in the flesh, so that we might grasp the idea of the unseen Father; and He endured the insolence of men, so that we might receive the inheritance of immortality."

Upward Mobility

"The ultimate end of the whole divine economy is the entry of God's creatures into the perfect unity of the Blessed Trinity" (CCC, no. 260). This is a family matter—that we are taken up, as sons and daughters, into the eternal relations of the Father, the Son, and the essence of love, the Holy Spirit. In Christ, we enter into the life of the Family Who is God. We begin that perfect communion in the same way God's people have always entered into relationship with God—the way that outsiders in the ancient world were brought into the trustee family. We enter the Family of God by means of a covenant.

Jesus declared this fact Himself, and at a supremely significant moment in His earthly life. Speaking on the night He was betrayed, mere hours before His arrest, He made it clear that He was laying down His life voluntarily, in a complete outpouring of love. He gave the apostles His Body, under the appearance of bread, and He gave them His blood, under the appearance of wine. All this took place in the context of the Passover meal, the covenant meal of ancient Israel. Yet Jesus emphasized that His self-donation, though prefigured in the sacrifice of the Passover lamb, constituted a *New Covenant*. Taking the cup of wine, He said, "This cup which is poured out for you is the New Covenant in My blood" (Lk 22:20).

In the hours and days that followed, He would indeed "pour out" Himself in a complete self-donation. The first Adam had faced sin and death and cowered in silent fear. The New Adam, however, faced sin and death—even the most humiliating and most painful death—and made death to die when He gave His life. Beginning with that Passover meal, Jesus would complete the self-sacrifice that Adam had refused. Whereas Adam failed to guard his household and failed to defend his beloved, Jesus succeeded on all counts, fulfilling every other intermediary covenant as well.

Unlike the old covenant(s), this was a family bond that would last forever, since *this* covenant consists of the very bond that holds the three divine Persons eternally in the perfect unity of the one and only God.

Sworn Again

So far as we know, Jesus used the term "New Covenant" only on that one occasion; but, for the first Christians, it came to define their new life. Moreover, it established their continuity with all the ancient family of God—from Adam through Noah, Abraham, Israel, Moses, and David. The New Covenant shared all the marks of the historic covenants and of the legal covenants of the trustee families. There was an oath, a sacrifice, and a shared meal. But the New Covenant brought all these elements to perfection. Now the oath was fulfilled; now the sacrifice was unblemished, and the priest and victim were God Himself; now the covenant was unbreakable, and the meal itself was a communion with God.

For the first Christians, the New Covenant, like all covenants, was a family affair. The Letter to the Hebrews discusses it in overwhelmingly familial terms such as "inheritance" and "firstborn." "Therefore [Jesus] is the mediator of a New Covenant, so that those who are called may receive the promised eternal inheritance, since a death has occurred which redeems them from the transgressions under the first covenant" (Heb 9:15). Remember that even the idea of "redemption" was a family matter, as the "redeemer" was the *go'el,* the one who avenged his kinfolk. "But you have come to Mount Zion and to the city of the living God . . . and to the assembly of the first-born" (Heb 12:22–23).

Incorporation into this family was not something theoretical, abstract, or merely spiritual. We *do* receive Jesus' Spirit (see Jn 20:22); otherwise we could not call God "Abba! Father!" (see Gal 4:6). But there is more at work in this New Covenant.

Re-flesh My Memory

From Jesus onward, the first Christians spoke of the covenant with flesh-and-blood realism. Implicitly contrasting the New Covenant with the old, Jesus said, at His next-to-last Passover, "It was not Moses who gave you the bread from heaven; My Father gives you the true bread from heaven. . . . I am the bread of life. . . . If any one eats of this bread, he will live for ever; and the bread which I shall give for the life of the world is My flesh" (Jn 6:32, 35, 51). This pointed forward to the covenant meal Jesus would serve at His final Passover.

St. Paul reports that, at that meal, Jesus commanded His disciples to "Do this"—to mark the covenant in the same way He had—"in remembrance of Me" (1 Cor 11:25). The Greek word that is translated here as "remembrance" carries much stronger connotations in ancient Hebrew culture. Given their original force, Paul's words evoke a "re-calling"—not only remembering but re-actualizing, re-presenting. This meal is unmistakably the Real Presence of Jesus Christ: Body, Blood, Soul, and Divinity. St. Paul elsewhere speaks of the covenant meal with the same vivid realism. "The cup of blessing which we bless, is it not a participation in the blood of Christ? The bread which we break, is it not a participation in the body of Christ?" (1 Cor 10:16). "Whoever, therefore, eats the bread or drinks the cup of the Lord in an unworthy manner will be guilty of profaning the body and blood of the Lord. . . . Any one who eats and drinks without discerning the body eats and drinks judgment upon himself" (1 Cor 11:27, 29).

In this New Covenant meal, we step beyond the shadows of metaphor into the very image and reality of God's glory. Our kinship with God is so real that His very blood courses through our bodies. We assimilate His flesh into our own. In the New Covenant meal, the Family of God eats the Body of Christ and so *becomes* the Body of Christ. This is how God willed us to become sons and daughters in the one eternal Son. "The children share in flesh and blood" (Heb 2:14), "conformed to the image of His Son" (Rom 8:29). By grace we are God's image and likeness, His blood kin.

A Close Call

Too little do Christians today realize the glory they receive in the New Covenant meal—the Eucharist, the Mass. This is unimaginable intimacy. A long-ago Christian from Thessalonica, Nicholas Cabasilas, wrote that Christ's "union with those whom He loves surpasses every union of which one might conceive." It is the closest family relation possible—closer than mother and child, closer than husband and wife, closer than twin siblings—and it binds a lowly human to Almighty God! Cabasilas goes so far as to say, "To whom else could one be more closely united than to oneself? Yet this very unity is inferior" to the union of God with the believer!

How can this be? In our communion of flesh and blood with Jesus, we receive the grace, the power, to live as He lives, to love as He loves, and so to give ourselves completely in self-donation for the sake of another—for the sake of Christ Himself. We receive the strength to live as Adam refused to live when he refused to die. For we receive the grace to live and die as Jesus lived and died. We can do this because now we live and die in Jesus. In laying down our lives as He laid down His life, we ourselves imitate the inner life of God, which is utter self-giving. "For whoever would save his life will lose it," Jesus said, "and whoever loses his life for My sake will find it" (Mt 16:25).

This life that we "find" is eternal, not merely everlasting, because it is God's own life. God alone is eternal. Rightly did the early Christians refer to "the new and eternal covenant." And rightly did the early Christians call our redemption a "new creation." For God Himself became a New Adam for our sake, and it is in *His* image and likeness that we are remade in baptism and Holy Communion, the two principal sacraments of His New Covenant.

When God first made man, He made us out of dust. Now He remakes us out of His own flesh and blood, and He makes us to share His "life-giving Spirit" (1 Cor 15:45). We, at last, are flesh of His flesh.

An Upward Fall

This was God's plan from the beginning, the plan that Adam had failed to complete. Yet we must be careful that we see the Original Sin rightly, for if we don't, we cannot see the Incarnation at all. It's not that God lost the first few rounds to the devil before sending His Son into the ring to win the match. God never loses. From the beginning He knew the end, and from the beginning He worked with that end in view.

In the beginning, He gave Adam freedom to offer himself up for the sake of his beloved. Without grace and freedom, Adam could not have truly given himself, he could not have loved, and he could not have imitated the inner life of the Trinity. Adam freely chose a lesser life, the life of a disobedient slave and not a son.

God knew, however, how He would restore His human family, in the fullness of time. He foretold it in stunning detail in the only Old Testament passage that refers to the New Covenant:

Behold, the days are coming, says the Lord, when I will make a new covenant with the house of Israel and the house of Judah, not like the covenant which I made with their fathers when I took them by the hand to bring them out of the land of Egypt, My covenant which they broke, though I was their husband, says the Lord. But this is the covenant which I will make with the house of Israel after those days, says the Lord: I will put My law within them, and I will write it upon their hearts; and I will be their God, and they shall be My people. And no longer shall each man teach his neighbor and each his brother, saying, "Know the Lord," for they shall all know Me, from the least of them to the greatest, says the Lord; for I will forgive their iniquity, and I will remember their sin no more. (Jer 31:31–34)

The New Covenant does not replace the old, but fulfills it, perfects it, and transforms it. Until we see all the old covenants in light of the Eucharistic reality of the New, we can't understand what happened in the beginning—nor can we see our destiny for all eternity.

CHAPTER 8

LIFE IN THE TRINITY

WITH THE NEW Covenant came a new way of living. It was clear, after all, that God's people would not keep the demands of the old covenant. Time after time, they had failed to live up to the promises; time after time, they had brought the covenant curses upon themselves. Something would have to change.

Jesus Himself spoke of this change at the beginning of His ministry, when He preached His Sermon on the Mount (see Mt 5). Six times in that sermon, He cited precepts of the old law: "You have heard that it was said to men of old . . ." But apparently, He cited these precepts only to contradict them. He concludes each citation with "But I say to you . . ."

Now, to contradict the law was an outrageous thing for a rabbi to do. The rabbis were ancient Israel's teachers and interpreters of the law, which Moses had received directly from God. It's an understatement to say that they tended to be modest and conservative in their preaching. Yet here came Jesus saying that the old law, which the nation had received from God, was no longer sufficient.

Since Israel had failed to keep up with the minimum standard of the old law, you might expect Jesus to demand much less with the new—to strike a covenant that would be easier to keep.

Yet nothing could be further from the truth of what He offered. Indeed, Jesus did *not* deny any of the precepts of the old law. Instead, He called His listeners to a still higher standard. He went beyond the old law, not against it.

"You have heard that it was said to the men of old, 'You shall not kill; and whoever kills shall be liable to judgment.' But I say to you that every one who is angry with his brother shall be liable to judgment; whoever insults his brother shall be liable to the council, and whoever says, 'You fool!' shall be liable to the hell of fire" (Mt 5:21–22).

That's amazing! God was no longer merely saying of sin, "Don't do it." Now, in Christ, He was saying, "Don't even *think* about it." This is especially remarkable when you consider the track record of God's covenant people. They'd had a hard enough time refraining from the *doing* of transgressions. Now came Jesus, calling them from the merely difficult to the clearly impossible.

In fact, in another, similar context, Jesus' audience brought up this very problem:

"When the disciples heard this, they were greatly astonished, saying, 'Who then can be saved?' But Jesus looked at them and said to them, 'With men this is impossible, but with God all things are possible'" (Mt 19:25–26).

The Gift Who Keeps on Giving

The law of the New Covenant is not only all-encompassing; it is all-consuming. It demands not only one's actions but one's thoughts and words—not only one's body but one's heart and mind and soul and spirit. In short, the New Covenant demands that people give precisely in the measure that God gives, which means that they give everything. The reward, however, is all-surpassing. The reward is to receive the very life of God, to love as God loves, with "His own glory and excellence" and "all things that pertain to life and godliness" (2 Pt 1:3). The reward for our total self-giving is God's total self-giving, in perfect and endless love and happiness. Only if we give as God gives may we live as God lives.

God wants us to be nothing less than "partakers of the divine nature" (2 Pt 1:4). But how can we do this? For us, the divine life does not "come naturally." We have a *human* nature, and *human* things come naturally to us. We eat, sleep, gather together, and mate without having to take extensive lessons beforehand. But the abundant life, perfect happiness—life in the Family of the Trinity—is not merely beyond our power; it is inconceivable to us.

Divine family life comes naturally only to the Trinity. Thus, for Jesus Christ, it comes naturally, since He is eternally "one in being with the Father." His nature is divine, and *only* He is God's Son by nature. So, if we are to become children of God by adoption, we must be remade in the image of Christ. Then the Father can see and love in us what He sees and loves in Christ. As we discussed in the preceding chapter, this remaking, this new creation, takes place through the sacraments. In these, we're raised *above our nature,* which is the very definition of "supernatural." For us mere mortals, divine life can only come as a supernatural gift, a grace, which is precisely what we receive in the sacraments.

In case you think I'm making all this up, I want to quote the Catholic Church's teaching on the subject, given in a recent document:

With Baptism we become children of God in His only-begotten Son, Jesus Christ. Rising from the waters of the baptismal font, every Christian hears again the voice that was once heard on the banks of the Jordan River: "You are my beloved Son; with You I am well pleased" (Lk 3:22). From this comes the understanding that one has been brought into association with the beloved Son, becoming a child of adoption (cf. Gal 4:4–7) and a brother or sister of Christ. In this way the eternal plan of the

Father for each person is realized in history: "For those whom He foreknew He also predestined to be conformed to the image of His Son, in order that He might be the firstborn among many brethren" (Rom 8:29).

To our heavenly Father we are more than just strangers who bear a striking resemblance to His Son. We are quite literally His children. Listen to St. Augustine, quoted in the same Church document: "Let us rejoice and give thanks; we have not only become Christians, but Christ Himself. . . . Stand in awe and rejoice: we have become Christ."

Remember, again, our discussion from the preceding chapter. Through the sacraments, you can enjoy a closer union with Christ than with any other person, including yourself! It is through this communion that we come to live divine communion with the Blessed Trinity.

Children of a Lesser Good

It is also through this communion that we receive the power to live according to the New Covenant. It is by God's "glory and excellence," "life and godliness," that we can live without sin, as Christ lived, for we live "in Christ" (see Eph 2:16) and Christ lives within us (see Gal 2:20).

Otherwise, what is to keep us from choosing as Adam chose? After all, we face the options he faced: to die

completely to ourselves and live forever in the Trinity, or
to live a little while longer on earth in our natural, mortal state.

We must not minimize this decision. What Adam
wanted was, in itself, good. In fact, it was very good. He
wanted safety and security. He wanted to preserve his life.
These are all good and noble objects. God Himself had
instilled the desire for them in human nature. What's
more, God had confirmed them in man by commanding
Adam to "guard" the Garden of Eden. To guard something is, by definition, to ensure its safety, security, and
preservation.

What Adam wanted, then, were good things. Yet they
were not the highest goods. They were not good
enough. The evil of Adam's sin was that he chose a lesser
good. He chose self-preservation over self-giving for the
sake of another. He preferred the gifts to the giver.

Choosing a lesser good, he chose a lesser life—and
spiritual death. By Adam's choice, God's creation stopped
far short of perfection. God had made him for divine life
in the Trinity; but Adam did not become all that God
had intended him to be, because he chose not to enact
God's life-giving love.

When Adam allowed himself to be governed by dread
instincts and proud passions, he knocked the whole human system out of whack. He chose to satisfy an urge, a
drive, an impulse, an instinct, rather than to act in good
faith. And that's what we choose whenever we choose to

sin. We opt for a momentary satisfaction instead of a lasting happiness. Ever since the Fall, we humans have been able to gain self-mastery only with great effort and difficulty, a little bit at a time.

Love Is a Battlefield

God fashioned all of us, as he fashioned Adam, with healthy desires for many things: food, sleep, sex, material resources, and the love and respect of other people (to name just a few). He made all these things to delight us. But, because of Adam's choice, our appetites for these goods are disordered—out of sync with reason and reality. We want more food than is good for us. We desire better shelter than we need to keep warm and dry. We desire more sex than the goals of marital communion and procreation require. It is this weakness that keeps our eyes trained on the earth, repeatedly choosing a quick fix for our cravings rather than eternal life in the Trinity.

The only way out is for us to discipline our appetites—again, not because the things we want are bad, but precisely because they're very good, yet we are inclined to put them to bad use. Created things are made to teach us about the creator. For example, we saw early in this book that marital communion is a natural analogy of the Trinitarian communion. So sex was meant to teach us about God and lead us to God. If, however, we treat sex or any other goods as ends in themselves, they can distract us from God and lead us to sin. As the saying goes, the road to hell is paved with good intentions, and we start down that road by choosing lesser natural goods over greater supernatural ones.

The classic definition describes *sin* as a turning away from God and toward creatures, toward a lesser good. Adam is not alone in making this choice. It's the choice we have all made. The Bible tells us that even the just man falls seven times a day (see Prv 24:16). And all our sins, whether great or small, further weaken us, disposing us to commit ever more sins.

This is the madness of our fall from grace. We choose trifles instead of the Trinity, fleeting pleasure rather than eternal life. It's completely irrational, but such is the state of people who follow their glandular promptings instead of reason aided by grace.

In the end, it's not a matter of forgoing sacrifice for the sake of earthly goods. For every choice demands a sacrifice. Every yes implies a corollary no: yes to this and no to that. So even our earthly loves will demand sacrifice from us. The only real choice we face is whether to sacrifice our bodily life for the sake of true love, or to sacrifice eternal life for the sake of pleasure here and now. If we choose the latter, we turn from God only to fall headlong into a whirlpool, to certain death.

And for what? The Russian novelist Fyodor Dostoyevsky

wrote of a revolutionary who was ready to betray his companions in order to gain a cigarette. That's where his nicotine addiction had driven him.

Yet that was Adam's choice, too. True love demanded his martyrdom, while disordered self-love urged him to save his hide. He chose his hide.

The constant tug of our own passions is in the same downward direction: toward self-gratification and away from self-giving. The revolutionary was willing to betray his comrades. Adam was willing to betray his bride. We should never underestimate our own weaknesses and the damage they can do.

Virtuous Reality

Even as we remain aware of our weaknesses, however, we must also build up our strength. We do this, first of all, through the sacraments, and also through cultivation of good habits, or virtues.

Holiness, or perfection in the Christian life, means conformity to the image of Jesus Christ. According to St. Paul, this is the condition of membership in the Family of God. "For those whom He foreknew He also predestined to be conformed to the image of His Son, in order that He might be the first-born among many brethren" (Rom 8:29).

In His earthly life, Jesus was "tempted as we are, yet without sin" (Heb 4:15). We, too—though we are often tempted—wish to be sinless like Christ, in order to live even now in the divine family. We need, then, to live as Jesus lived, first by receiving His life in Holy Communion and then by imitating His life in our every thought, word, and deed. The first of the means to this life—the sacraments—strengthens us for the second: the habits of virtue.

With us, virtue may seem impossible, "but with God all things are possible." It can help us to think of our growth in Christian life, as the early Christians did, as a process of growing up—"until we all attain . . . to mature manhood, to the measure of the stature of the fullness of Christ" (Eph 4:13).

Our life in Christ forms us for the self-giving love that is at the heart of the Trinitarian family. We can see how this gradual self-denial goes along with maturation even in earthly families.

Family life begins when a man and woman marry. In marriage, each spouse gradually gives up preferences, peeves, privacy, and personal space in order to share life with his or her beloved. It's a slow process, and it doesn't always come easily. Moreover, before the process is complete, the starry-eyed couple must be ready to look beyond their self-enclosed world to care for a child. The child, for his part, is only beginning his process of maturation, and cries for the satisfaction of his most immediate needs: to be fed, warmed, changed, jostled.

But love does a remarkable thing in a good home. The individual, the couple, the baby, gradually become conformed to *the family,* precisely by their gift of self.

Domestic peace depends upon every individual's adaptation to the family home. Dysfunction is what happens when one or more individuals don't adapt and consistently choose themselves above others.

Deferred gratification, then, is a hallmark of maturity. An infant cannot conceive of such a deferral. We measure the baby's development, in part, by his ability to wait for life's good and necessary things. The family's peace depends on his learning those lessons.

Yet the young couple, too, have to learn those lessons. First as individuals and then as a couple, they must learn that their own happiness must be subsumed into a larger happiness, the family's happiness. Moreover, they must learn that their individual happiness is inconceivable apart from the family's happiness. If they learn their lessons well, they will find that they are happiest when making others happy.

Said St. Cyril of Alexandria, "The willingness to serve is what invites us to freedom and the honor that is the special privilege of sons; but disobedience humbles us to a base and shameful servitude, if it is true, as it certainly is, that everyone who commits sin is a slave to sin" (see Rom 6).

In the Pourhouse

Self-giving marks the way of integration into any family. In the Trinitarian family, this is true to the ultimate degree.

From this we may discern the morality implicit in our

life as children of God. We deny ourselves—our desires, our urges, our drives, our inclinations—in imitation of Christ. We pour ourselves out in imitation of God. We take up our cross *daily* and follow Him. It's not a onetime decision. We must make the self-offering every morning and renew it with every action of the body and every motion of the heart and mind. God lives His self-donation completely, eternally, all at once. We, in time and space, must do it incrementally, little by little. St. Irenaeus put it poetically: "By this arrangement . . . man, a created and organized being, is rendered after the image and likeness of the uncreated God, . . . making progress day by day, and ascending towards the perfect, that is, approximating to the uncreated One. For the Uncreated is perfect, that is, God."

Self-denial, then, is not a mask for self-contempt, but the necessary means for achieving self-mastery; and self-mastery makes possible our self-giving and self-fulfillment. Sin, according to this view, is not wanting too much, but settling for too little! It's settling for self-gratification rather than self-fulfillment.

We take possession of ourselves so that we can give ourselves away, so that we can become ourselves. This is the essence of our Trinitarian life. If it is to become our own family life, we must live up to it. We need to be made into Christ, so that we can give ourselves to the Father in true freedom, unimpeded, unencumbered, without attachments to earthly loves or earthly goods, and without Adam's weakness. The moral life is our gradual perfection in this communion, fitting us for heaven, even now on earth.

Simon Says: Live Like God

In our discussion throughout this chapter, I've quoted from the first chapter of the Second Letter of Peter. Few passages in the Bible convey the terms of the New Covenant with such force and clarity. In just a few verses, we see it all: the power of grace, the divine life, the promises of the covenant, the effects of Adam's sin, the remedy for our weakness, our family relations, and the ultimate reward.

Simon Peter knew the life we were made for: life in the Trinity. Let's take it in now all at once:

His divine power has granted to us
all things that pertain to life and godliness,
through the knowledge of Him who called us
to His own glory and excellence,
by which He has granted to us
His precious and very great promises,
that through these you may escape from the corruption
that is in the world because of passion,
and become partakers of the divine nature.
For this very reason make every effort
to supplement your faith with virtue,

and virtue with knowledge,
and knowledge with self-control,
and self-control with steadfastness,
and steadfastness with godliness,
and godliness with brotherly affection,
and brotherly affection with love. . . .
Therefore, brethren, be the more zealous
to confirm your call and election,
for if you do this you will never fall;
so there will be richly provided for you
an entrance into the eternal kingdom
of our Lord and Savior Jesus Christ. (2 Pet 1:3–7, 10–11)

CHAPTER 9

AT HOME IN THE CHURCH

JESUS SAID A strange thing just before He went to His passion and death. He told His disciples, "I will not leave you orphans" (Jn 14:18). Some translations render the last word as "desolate," but the Greek word is *orphanous*, which means, literally, a child without either father or mother. In the ancient world, orphans were those who had no family to care for them, no place to live. They were desolate, outcast by circumstance, the poorest of the poor.

Since Jesus was going away, He knew the anxieties His disciples would feel. For three years, He had been family to them—a father figure, a patriarch, an elder brother. He wanted to assure them that He would not leave them homeless or without a family.

That's a thoughtful sentiment, but rather odd coming from Someone Who had taught people to call God "Father," and Who would later tell them, "I am with you always, to the close of the age" (Mt 28:20). If God was their Father, and Jesus, their brother, was always with them, why should those first Christians ever consider themselves orphans? Why would they need such assurance from Jesus?

Hey Judea

Consider for a moment what was about to happen to Jesus' disciples. Not only would their Master be taken from them, sacrificed on the cross, only to rise again and ascend into heaven, but within a generation the world as they knew it would crumble to dust. Remember that the Tribe of Judah, though subject to Rome, had remained a single family unit, history's most enduring and successful trustee family. The Judeans, the Jews, were united by bonds of blood and covenant. All the lives of the descendants of Israel were circumscribed by their place in the family and the demands of the covenant. The trustee family defined the trade they plied, the lands they inhabited, the wars they fought, and the sacrifices they offered to God. As individuals, the Jews could not conceive of themselves apart from their kin. As kin, they could not conceive of themselves apart from the covenant, which defined their family membership.

Yet all this would soon pass away, and Jesus knew it would. In A.D. 70, just forty years after Jesus' ascension, the Roman emperor Titus's armies laid waste to Jerusalem, destroying the Temple and scattering the people.

We must not underestimate the devastation this brought, not only to Judea but to each and every Jew. This was the end not only of their nationalistic hopes but of their way of life and worship, their culture, and their family identity, which was their most fundamental identity before God. Jerusalem was more than the Judean capital and a pilgrimage site. Old Jerusalem was a *mother* to all Israelites—a *metropolis,* the word that in Greek means "mother city" (see 2 Sm 20:19).

Thus, Jesus needed to assure those first Christians—who were Israelites, too—that they would always have a home, that there would be a New Covenant, that though the trustee family was passing away, a greater one would rise in its place. He would not leave them orphans.

One Bride, One Body

Without the Promised Land, then, what would be their home? Apart from the Temple, where would God's people offer sacrifice? Where would they seal and renew the family covenant?

These were the key questions for the first generation of Christians. In their New Testament writings, the apostles Paul, Peter, John, and James concerned themselves, to a great extent, with establishing the continuity between God's New Covenant family and His "first-born," Israel. As good Israelites, they took care to establish the terms of family life in the New Covenant. They knew that, without such terms, there could be no covenant.

The old covenants had gradually extended God's family to more people on earth, but they had also anticipated a covenant by which God's household would reach *all* people. God swore to Abraham, "by your descendants shall *all* the nations of the earth bless themselves" (Gn 22:18). The prophet Isaiah foretold a day when "the house of the Lord shall be established as the highest of the mountains, and shall be raised above the hills; and *all* the nations shall flow to it" (Is 2:2). The prophet Malachi shared the same vision, of a day when, "from the rising of the sun to its setting [God's] name is great among the nations, and in every place incense is offered to [His] name, and a pure offering" (Mal 1:11).

The place of this offering, according to Jesus, was to be His Church. He told His disciples, "On this rock," meaning Peter, "I will build my Church" (Mt 16:18). For the apostles, then, the Church became Christ's living legacy—the place where His one sacrifice would be offered in every place on earth, from sunrise to sunset. The Church would be the place of the Eucharist, the place of baptism. For Christians, the Church would be home, the place of the covenant—which, after all, is sealed by baptism and renewed in the Eucharist.

Throughout the New Testament, the apostles wax mystical when they speak of the Church, and no one more so than St. Paul, who expressly called it a "mystery" (Eph 5:32). How great is this mystery? It is so great that the angels in heaven must learn the wisdom of God from the Church and through the Church (see Eph 3:10).

Yet this is the Church made up of people like you and me. Throughout his letters, St. Paul used two images in describing the Church: It is Christ's Bride, and it is His Body. By now, you should not be surprised to learn that the two images, together, make sense only in the context of the first chapters of the Book of Genesis. Indeed, Paul even quotes the passage from Genesis that reconciles these two seemingly contradictory images: "For this reason a man shall leave his father and mother and be joined to his wife, and the two shall become one flesh" (Eph 5:31; Gn 2:24). When Adam saw Eve, he exclaimed that she, at last, was "bone of my bones and flesh of my flesh" (Gn 2:23). And that is what Christ says when He looks upon the Church, His Bride, who assimilates Him in the communion of the Eucharist. As John testified, "I saw the holy city, new Jerusalem, coming down out of heaven from God, prepared as a bride adorned for her husband" (Rv 21:2).

In sum, Paul wasn't mixing his metaphors; the Church is the Bride and Body of Christ, as Eve was Adam's bride and flesh-and-bone body.

Through the Church, then, God provides the moment that all creation has been longing for, since God first created man. In the Church, God gave Israel and the Gentiles a trustee family and a kingdom that would last forever, faithful to its covenants.

No Church, No Father

In baptism, the Church gives new birth to believers, and so the Church is also called "mother." Again, this does not contradict the Church's status as "bride." Recall that the union between Christ and believers is so strong that it surpasses all analogies with earthly experiences of family. This is not to say that it abolishes those analogies; rather, it fulfills them, one and all. The Church loves as both a mother and a bride. The prophet Isaiah foresaw this, too, when he said to Israel, "You shall no more be termed Forsaken . . . but you shall be called 'My delight is in her,' and your land 'Married.' For as a young man marries a virgin, so shall your sons marry you, and as the bridegroom rejoices over the bride, so shall your God rejoice over you" (Is 62:4–5).

The early Christians loved the Church for its motherhood. Writing in the second and third centuries, Tertullian of Carthage referred to "Lady Mother Church." In the next generation, the great St. Cyprian declared, "He cannot have God for His Father who refuses to have the Church for His mother." Elsewhere, he added, "She is one mother, plentiful in fruitfulness. From her womb we are born, by her milk we are nourished, by her spirit we are animated."

Just as Christ had promised in His farewell discourse to His disciples, He would not leave them orphans. He left them a Church to be their mother. And the union between the Church and believers is even closer than the union between a pregnant mother and her baby, between a nursing mother and her newborn. In the Church, believers are bound in the closest bond with one another and with Christ the bridegroom. In the Church, Christians live fully in Christ, through the power of His sacraments—and so they enjoy the life of the Trinity, heaven itself, even on earth.

This Functional Family

The Family of God also provides an intimate experience of brotherhood and sisterhood in the Communion of Saints, which is the Church's covenant family extended through time and space. "Becoming a disciple of Jesus means accepting the invitation to belong to *God's family*" (CCC, no. 2233). In this context, we can understand the care of the saints in heaven for people on earth, and we can understand the care of the Church on earth for the souls of the faithful departed, who are undergoing purification for life in heaven. For the members of the Church are siblings in a close-knit family.

In the supernatural family of the saints, Mary holds an eminent place. Of all creatures, only Mary is directly related to God by a natural bond of covenant kinship. She is the Mother of Jesus, to Whom she gave her own flesh and blood. This bond enabled humankind to share the grace of Christ by adoption. Thus, as brothers and sisters of Christ, Christians are also children of Mary, and so are bound to honor her as their mother. Furthermore, Jesus Himself is legally bound by His Father's law ("Honor your father and mother") to share His honor with Mary. Indeed, He fulfilled this law more perfectly than any son has ever done, by bestowing the gift of His divine glory upon Mary. Christians, in turn, are called to imitate Him in this way, as in all other ways.

Thus, no matter what sort of family we've come from—no matter what sort of dysfunction we've known—it is in the Church that we can begin again in a home that is heavenly. It is there that we find siblings: our brothers and sisters, both living and dead, in the Communion of Saints. It is in the Church that we find true fathers: in the priests in our parish, as well as the ancient patriarchs who established the faith for us. It is in the Church that we return to our mother, who waits with open arms and the milk of consolation. In the Church of Jesus Christ, no one is an orphan.

There's No Place Like Rome

Baptized in water and the Spirit, all of us are brothers and sisters in the family of Jesus Christ. The early Christians—even those who were not Jews—knew this to be so. The Romans who accepted the Gospel faced no immediate threat to their trustee family, but they knew that they now belonged, by covenant, to another family, a larger family, a divine family. Many wealthy Roman families gave their homes over to become "house churches," where the Mass was offered. They replaced the portraits of their pagan ancestors with portraits of their new ancestors: the biblical patriarchs, the apostles, and the saints.

For this reason, some Romans who remained pagan saw the Church as a threat to traditional family life. A man or woman who converted to Christianity could no longer worship the household gods, could no longer tend the shrine of the ancestors. The Church did not, however, come to abolish the institution of the family, but to perfect it, to make it universal. For the institution could not survive in its merely natural state.

By establishing the New Covenant, Christ founded one Church—His Mystical Body—as an extension of His Incarnation. By taking on flesh, Christ divinized flesh, and He extended the Trinity's life to all humanity through the Church, the Family of God. Incorporated into the Body of Christ, Christians become "sons in the Son." They become children in the eternal household of God. They share the family life of the Trinity.

The familial theme that dominates Scripture continued through the earliest centuries of the Church. St.

Polycarp of Smyrna, in the generation immediately after the apostles, wrote, "For if we continue to love one another and to join in praising the Most Holy Trinity—all of us who are sons of God and form one family in Christ—we will be faithful to the deepest vocation of the Church" (see CCC, no. 959).

This is as true today as it was for the first Christians. The very first point of the *Catechism of the Catholic Church* states that God "calls together all men, scattered and divided by sin, into the unity of His family, the Church" (no. 1). Elsewhere, the *Catechism* says that "the Church is nothing other than 'the family of God'" (no. 1655). And this family is not only global but also local. Pope John Paul II wrote that "the great family which is the Church . . . finds concrete expression in the diocesan and the parish family. . . . No one is without a family in this world: the Church is a home and family for everyone."

The earthly household of the Trinity is this universal Family of God, outside of which there is no salvation (CCC, no. 846). That's a strong statement, and it makes some people wince. But this teaching does not condemn anyone. It simply clarifies the essential meaning of salvation and the Church. Since the essence of salvation is divine family life, the life of divine sonship, to speak of salvation outside God's Family, the Church, is to confuse things greatly. Being *outside* God's Family is precisely what people need to be saved from! Non-Catholic Christians are, however, considered "separated brethren," united to God's Family by the sacrament of baptism. The *Catechism* states this truth in moving terms: "All who have been justified by faith in baptism . . . are accepted as brothers in the Lord by the children of the Catholic Church" (no. 818). We can rejoice in this mercy, even as we strive to bring all our siblings into fuller communion.

Role Call

Within the Church, as within the natural family, there are clearly defined roles. From the time of the apostles, the Christian faithful have viewed the clergy as spiritual fathers. Indeed, even in the Old Testament, priests were identified this way. In the Book of Judges, when the Levite appears at Micah's door, Micah pleads, "Stay with me, and be to me a father and a priest" (17:10). In the New Testament, then, St. Paul clearly sees his role as paternal: "For I became your father in Christ Jesus through the Gospel" (1 Cor 4:15; see also 1 Jn 2:13–14). The great earthly father of the Church is, of course, the "Holy Father," the Pope—a word that comes from the Italian *papa*.

We see this family spirit in every generation, as long as there have been Christians. For St. Ignatius of Antioch—who lived in the generation of the apostles—the divine family, the Trinity, was the model of concord in the Church: "Be obedient to your bishop and to one another, as Jesus Christ in His human nature was subject to the Father and as the Apostles were to Christ and the Father. In this way there will be union of body and spirit." And elsewhere he wrote, "I congratulate you who are closely attached to [your bishop] as the Church is attached to Jesus Christ and as Jesus Christ to the Father, that all may be in harmonious unity."

St. Jerome, in the fourth century, wrote, "Be obedient to your bishop and welcome him as the father of your soul."

Perhaps the greatest of the Church Fathers (a term that in itself is significant) was St. Augustine, and from him we learn: "The apostles were sent as fathers; to replace those apostles, sons were born to you who were constituted bishops. . . . The Church calls them fathers, she who gave birth to them, who placed them in the sees of their fathers. . . . Such is the Catholic Church. She has given birth to sons who, through all the earth, continue the work of her first fathers."

The Church is one as the Trinity is one. Our earthly unity is God the Father's answer to the prayer of His Son: "that they may all be one; even as You, Father, are in Me, and I in You, that they also may be in Us, so that the world may believe that You have sent Me. The glory which You have given Me I have given to them, that they may be one even as We are one, I in them and You in Me, that they may become perfectly one, so that the world may know that You have sent Me and have loved them even as You have loved Me" (Jn 17:21–23). The Church is one in the Spirit, Whose coming is itself the fulfillment of Jesus' high-priestly prayer.

CHAPTER 10

THE FAMILY SPIRIT

THE CHURCH IS our mother, and for that we
should rejoice. Moreover, Jesus Christ has given
us His own mother, Mary, to be our mother,
too. Praise God for that—because if He has given us His
mother as our own, He will surely deny us nothing! It almost seems an understatement to say He has not left us
orphans. His gifts surely surpass all of humankind's ex-
pectations for salvation.

Yet there is something penultimate in these gifts of
motherhood. Great as they are, they point to a still
greater gift Our Lord wants to give us.

The Great Unknown

In this chapter, I'd like to search out the identity of the
Holy Spirit. For Christians today, the Person of the Spirit
has proved to be the most elusive of the Blessed

Trinity—so elusive that one modern saint called the Holy Spirit "the Great Unknown."

After all, when we approach the Father, we can relate to Him as to someone we know on earth, someone familiar—and familial. He is a father. In the same way, when we approach the Son, we can relate to Him as an elder brother, for that is how He revealed Himself. Again, our relationship is familiar and familial.

But how can we relate to the Holy Spirit? We meditate on the usual litany of titles and images from the Bible, and we come up with . . . what? Holy Wind, Holy Breath, Holy Fire, Holy Dove. But nothing—or, rather, no One—we can relate to in a familiar and familial way.

Now, don't get me wrong. If we're only supposed to imagine the Spirit through impersonal images such as these, we should be content. After all, this is the realm of deepest mystery. So how dare we presume to go prying into God's inner life?

But that's just the point. We aren't presuming or prying. We're simply opening up the gift that a loving God has given. We're simply taking our Father at His Word, as trusting children, so that we can better receive and appreciate that gift—of His Spirit.

Don't forget how long God's people had been waiting for this gift, based on God's promise repeatedly made by the prophets to ancient Israel. It was restated at the start of Jesus' ministry (Mt 3:11–16; Jn 1:31–33) and then again—most emphatically—at the end (Jn 14–16).

Taking "It" Personally

Right before his final departure and return to the Father, Jesus declared to His disciples, "I will pray the Father, and He will give you another Counselor, to be with you for ever, even the Spirit of truth" (Jn 14:16–17). Then Jesus assured them with a solemn promise: "I will not leave you orphans."

When the disciples heard that Jesus was about to leave and return to the Father, forever, they must have started wondering whether they were about to become spiritual orphans. To assure them otherwise, Jesus offered them real comfort and consolation. And Who better than a divine Person known as the Comforter and Consoler?

Precisely how, then, does the Spirit keep us from becoming "orphans"? Is there a family relationship we have been missing in this modern age?

I believe there is, and that Scripture and Sacred Tradition lead us to discover it. I must emphasize, however, that our explorations must be cautious, and any observations or opinions tentative. Here especially, as in all things, we must submit our findings to the Church for judgment. Indeed, if the Magisterium should find any of them to be unsatisfactory, I will be the first to renounce them, and rip the following pages out of the book and gratefully consign them to the flames—and then invite you to do the same.

Motherwise Known As . . .

Just as we came to know *Who* the first two Persons are, as Father and Son, by *what* They did—when the Father sent the Son among us—so it is with the Holy Spirit. We discover *Who* the third Person is by *what* the Spirit does.

For instance, Jesus identifies the Spirit as the divine agent of our rebirth as God's children in baptism: "Unless one is born of water and the Spirit, he cannot enter the kingdom of God" (Jn 3:5). Our supernatural birth and first bath are *what* the Holy Spirit does. Likewise, Paul describes how our own "adoption as sons" is associated with the Holy Spirit, and the "groaning in travail" that accompanies "the redemption of our bodies" (Rom 8:22–23).

Following the birth pangs of the Holy Spirit's labor and delivery of God's "children," Paul and Peter both urge us, as "babes in Christ," to "long for the pure spiritual milk" (1 Cor 3:1–3; 1 Pt 2:2). Likewise, the Spirit is the one who teaches us to walk and talk ("walk by the Spirit," Gal 5:16; "pray . . . in the Spirit," Eph 6:18). Only then can "the fruit of the Spirit" mature (Gal 5:22).

How fitting it is, then, that one of the first words the

Spirit teaches God's little ones is "Abba," as Paul explains: "When we cry, 'Abba! Father!' it is the Spirit Himself bearing witness with our spirit that we are children of God" (Rom 8:16). In other words, the Spirit helps us to recognize—and call upon—God as "Abba, Father," much as my wife Kimberly taught our six kids not to be afraid of that tall, dark figure with the deep voice—but to call me "Daddy."

And the Spirit's work doesn't stop with the first few words. As humbling as it is, "the Spirit helps us in our weakness; for we do not [even] know how to pray as we ought," and so the Spirit "intercedes for us with sighs too deep for words" (Rom 8:26).

I read and apply all of this as a child of God, but also as a father of six. And it fits Kimberly to a tee. That's why my kids have no trouble grasping what I mean when I call their mom the Holy Spirit of our home. Thus, they also understand the double application of Paul's teaching, "Don't grieve the Holy Spirit" (Eph 4:30). Indeed, through years of experience, they know why blaspheming the Holy Spirit is treated differently than every other sin and blasphemy (Mt 12:31–32), by their earthly and heavenly fathers. Dad's first law is: You'd better not make Mom mad.

For me, all of this serves to reinforce the Holy Spirit's motherly role as comforter and consoler, just as Jesus promised that he wouldn't leave us orphans (Jn 14:16–18). Thus, what a mother does in the natural order, the Holy Spirit accomplishes in the supernatural order. What earthly mothers do finitely and inchoately, the Spirit accomplishes infinitely and perfectly.

In sum, as our mothers gave us birth, so the Spirit gives us rebirth. As a mother feeds her children, so the Spirit feeds the children of God with spiritual milk. As a mother groans in labor, so the Spirit groans to give us life. Interestingly, the Greek verb for "groan" in Romans 8:22 is the same term used to describe the birth pangs in the story of Adam and Eve (Gn 3:16). There is resonance in other parts of the Old Testament as well.

Speaking Words of Wisdom

In the Book of Wisdom (chapters 7–9), God's Wisdom is referred to as "holy spirit," and then described in terms that are both strikingly *divine* ("all-powerful," "all-knowing," 7:22–23) and *feminine* ("irresistible," "more beautiful than the sun," 7:22, 29).

The book portrays Israel's sage-king praising Wisdom as a most radiant mother: "The Spirit of wisdom came to me. . . . I loved her . . . and I chose to have her. . . . because her radiance never ceases. All good things came to me along with her. . . . because wisdom leads them; but I did not know that she was their mother" (Wis 7:7, 10–12).

God's Spirit is identified with Wisdom, and Wisdom is then personified as eternal and maternal and *bridal*. Thus, for Solomon, Lady Wisdom is the only true object of his passion: "I loved her and sought her from my youth, and I desired to take her for my bride, and I became enamored of her beauty" (Wis 8:2). Indeed, as Solomon grew older, his desire for Wisdom only grew stronger: "Therefore I determined to take her to live with me, knowing that she would give me good counsel and encouragement in cares and grief" (Wis 8:9).

More than comfort, Solomon wanted to be intimate and to sleep with her: "When I enter my house, I shall take my repose beside her" (Wis 8:16). This was not to satisfy his lust, but to discover, "in friendship with her, pure delight" (Wis 8:17).

Nowhere else in Scripture do we find such an elaborate description of Wisdom. So what are we to make of this scriptural figure of Lady Wisdom?

Benedict Ashley, O.P., notices how Wisdom is applied elsewhere to God's law (Sir 24) and to Jesus (1 Cor 1:24). "Yet more properly," Ashley concludes, "it is to the Third Person of the Trinity . . . who is Love, wise Love, that the Old Testament descriptions of a feminine Wisdom are applied." This conclusion seems very reasonable.

More still may be implicit in other parts of the Old Testament, as even the ancient rabbis observed. In Hebrew, *ruah,* the word for "spirit"—as in the Spirit of God that hovered above the waters (Gn 1:2)—is a feminine noun. Another common Old Testament image for the Spirit is the *shekinah,* or "glory cloud," that filled the

Holy of Holies in the Jerusalem Temple. *Shekinah,* too, is a feminine noun. For many rabbis, these usages were sufficient evidence for the bridal-maternal character of God's Spirit.

Soul Provider

In the preceding chapter, we spoke of the Church as the Body of Christ and the Bride of Christ. The Church is the New Eve to Christ, Who is the New Adam. From Whom, then, does this Bride and Body receive her identity, her life?

St. John indicates that the Church received its life when Jesus breathed upon His disciples and said, "Receive the Holy Spirit" (Jn 20:22). It is the Holy Spirit Who gives life to Christ's Mystical Body, the Church. Indeed, Sacred Tradition refers to the Spirit as the "soul of the Mystical Body." In the words of Pope Leo XIII: "as Christ is the Head of the Church, so is the Holy Ghost her soul." He goes on to quote St. Augustine: "As the soul is in our body, so the Holy Spirit is in Christ's Body, the Church."

Without the soul, your body would be a corpse. So likewise with the Spirit and the Church.

Moreover, the soul is, by definition, the form of the body. It is what gives life to the body; it is the essence, what we might call the identity, of the person. To paraphrase Pope John Paul II: The soul forms the body, just as the body reveals the soul (see also CCC, no. 365). Thus, in human beings, biological maleness and femaleness express not just biological differences but a fundamental reality in the soul.

The Holy Spirit is the soul of the Mystical Body. However, the Church is a spiritual body, and so we cannot speak of it as male or female, even though Tradition refers to it as Bride and Mother. Similarly, God is transcendent, and so we may not speak of God as having "masculine or feminine qualities," even though the first two divine Persons are properly named Father and Son.

We may, however, ask what the Body—in this case the Church—reveals or expresses about the soul—in this case the Spirit.

The Mother Lode

Tradition shows us that the Church's bridal-maternity may itself be a participation in the life of the divine family.

All perfections are contained in the God we call Father, and this is no less true of perfect motherhood. The great theologian Cardinal Yves M. J. Congar saw this as a necessary corollary to the narrative of Genesis: "God created man in His own image, in the image of God He created him; male and female He created them" (Gn 1:27). Congar concluded that "there must be in God, in a transcendent form, something that corresponds to masculinity and something that corresponds to femininity."

No less a doctrinal authority than Cardinal Joseph Ratzinger has echoed Congar: "Because of the teaching about the Spirit, one can as it were practically have a presentiment of the primordial type of the feminine, in a mysterious, veiled manner, within God Himself."

The idea did not, however, originate with Cardinals Congar and Ratzinger. In fact, some of the greatest of the ancient Fathers, especially in the Syriac tradition (St. Ephrem, Aphrahat, Narsai), associated a "divine maternity" with the person of the Holy Spirit.

Roman Catholics profess in the Nicene Creed that the Holy Spirit "proceeds from the Father and the Son." St. Methodius of Olympus saw this dual "procession" reflected as man was created in the divine image. As Eve proceeded from her Father God and from the side of His son Adam, so the Spirit proceeds from both the Father and the eternal Son. As the Father made Eve from the rib of Adam, so Methodius called the Holy Spirit the "rib of the Word"—the uncreated principle of maternity.

Sainted Samples

Beyond Scripture, we find further instances of the Spirit's maternity in Sacred Tradition. This understanding continued in the Church through the patristic period (see Sources and References at the end of the book) and the Middle Ages, when St. Catherine of Siena said, "The Holy Spirit becomes [for people who abandon themselves to Providence] a mother who feeds them from the breast of divine charity."

In the twentieth century, St. Maximilian Kolbe, who was martyred by the Nazis, spoke of a special relationship between the Holy Spirit and Mary, the Mother of Jesus. "They share," he wrote, "a single motherhood: the divine Maternity of love." Mary is traditionally called the Immaculate Conception because from the moment of conception she was preserved from sin. Kolbe taught that this quality, too, was a reflection of the Holy Spirit, Whom he called the "uncreated immaculate conception." Mary, he went on, "was created on purpose to show by her virginal motherhood the presence of the Holy Spirit in her." Kolbe was even so bold as to say that Mary was like an incarnation ("quasi-incarnatus") of the Holy Spirit.

Another recent witness to these truths is St. Edith Stein, a Jewish convert and philosopher who, like Kolbe, died in a Nazi concentration camp. She wrote, "In this womanhood devoted to the service of love, is there really a divine image? Indeed, yes. . . . Such love is properly the attribute of the Holy Spirit. Thus we can see the prototype of the feminine being in the Spirit of God poured over all creatures. It finds its perfect image in the purest Virgin who is the bride of God and mother of all mankind."

The Spirit and the Church converge most perfectly in the Mother of God. As in the Western tradition Mary is often called the "archetype of the Church," so the East refers to her as both an "icon of the Church" and an "icon of the Spirit." Now, an icon is more than a "picture"; it is a window onto a heavenly reality. It is the Blessed Virgin, then, who opens our view onto the eternal life of the Spirit—even as she manifests the Body to which the Spirit gives life: the Church. Mary's maternity is mystically one with that of the Church and the Spirit.

The Bridal Path

The Church shows a character that is bridal as well as maternal, and this, too, is an expression of her eternal soul, the Holy Spirit. The Spirit's bridal associations are clear in the Book of Wisdom (chapters 7–9), and also in the rabbis' interpretations of scriptural texts such as the Song of Songs. How fitting, for example, that the Hebrew word for "marriage" is *kiddushin,* a word that also means "holiness"—a gift we receive from the Spirit.

Divine revelation itself culminates in the Book of Revelation—the *Apokalypsis,* or "Unveiling." The Apocalypse shows the consummation of salvation history to be a nuptial banquet, "the marriage supper of the Lamb" (Rv 19:7, 9). Then all of Scripture draws to a close with an invitation spoken at once by the Church and the Holy Spirit: "The Spirit and the Bride say, 'Come!'" (Rv 22:17).

As we've seen again and again, we learn Who God is

from what God does—from the works of creation and revelation. Thus, what we said earlier of the Trinity in general, we apply here to the Persons of the Godhead: By divine actions that are bridal and maternal, we may come to discern a divine bridal-maternity in the Holy Spirit.

Still Our Father

I must raise a caution here. This does not mean that we call God "Mother"; divine revelation does not call God by that name. Nor is it found anywhere in the Church's living Tradition. Ironically, to do so, on account of the Spirit, would be to undermine the very work of that same Spirit, Who is intent upon teaching us to address— and come to know—God as "Abba, Father."

Nor do I mean to imply that there are masculine or feminine qualities within the Godhead. Again, there are no bodily features of gender and sexuality in the Trinity. At most, human forms of physical gender and sexuality are reflections of the purely immaterial relations unique to each member of the Trinity. It is in the relations of the human family that the life of the Trinity is reflected more truly and fully than anywhere else in the natural order. In other words, the analogy of bridal-motherhood here is *relational* and *familial,* not *physical* or *sexual* (much less political). Thus, there is no more justification for goddess worship today than there was when the prophets condemned it in ancient Israel.

Let Us Proceed

Some might object that this familial understanding (or "social analogy") of the relations of the Trinity clashes with the traditional "psychological" analogy proposed by the two greatest lights of the Western theological tradition, St. Augustine and St. Thomas Aquinas. That analogy is most simply and clearly summarized by the lay apologist Frank Sheed:

> *The First Person knows Himself; His act of knowing Himself produces an Idea, a Word; and this Idea, this Word, the perfect Image of Himself, is the Second Person. The First Person and the Second combine in an act of love—love of one another, love of the glory of the Godhead which is their own; and just as the act of knowing produces an Idea within the Divine Nature, the act of loving produces a state of Lovingness within the Divine Nature. Into this Lovingness, Father and Son pour all that they have and all that they are, with no diminution, nothing held back. Thus the Lovingness within the Godhead is utterly equal to the Father and the Son, for they have poured their all into it. . . . Thus their Lovingness too is Infinite, Eternal, Living, Someone, a Person, God.*

There are two "processions" within the Trinity: The Father generates the Son, and the Spirit proceeds from the Father and the Son. The traditional model understands the first procession to be a matter of the mind of God, an "intellectual" procession of knowing, and the second procession to be a matter of the will of God, a "volitional" procession of loving. The second procession flows from the first, since one can only love what one knows.

How does this relate to family life? To know someone truly, and to love whom we know: This is the very essence of family life; it's the essence of the Church's life; and it's the essence of God's life.

Home Is Where the Heart (and Head) Are

We can learn still more of this eternal, divine life by examining what God does for us on earth. Consider, for example, the two dimensions of our salvation that St. Paul so emphasized: justification and sanctification. These represent two dimensions of our experience of God that correspond to the two eternal processions in God. We can look at salvation in legal terms, as justice, obedience, and keeping the Father's law. We see our justification, then, as a work of the Son, the Logos—because it is a work understood in legal and rational terms. We may also, however, look upon our salvation in terms of sanctification—a free gift of love, a grace dispensed ordinarily through communal and sacramental worship. We can describe our sanctification, then, as a work of the Holy Spirit, the Sanctifier—and a work that is bridal-maternal in nature.

Knowledge and love are perfected eternally in one indivisible act. We see this divine reality expressed in creation—in salvation history, in the life of the Church, and in our own lives. We can't love what we don't know, but we can sometimes know in an unloving way. Law without love leaves us with coldhearted intellectualism. Love without law, on the other hand, is debased, degenerate.

Law is ordered to love, and love perfects the law. St. Paul tells us that "knowledge puffs up, but love builds up" (1 Cor 8:1). Yet Paul is not advocating blissful ignorance, for he also urges us to speak the truth in love (Eph 4:15). We need both together, knowledge and love, in order to live in the image and likeness of the triune God. Thus, we need both together, knowledge and love, if we are to be fully human. Salvation, in the end, means becoming truly human, fulfilling the deepest needs of knowing and loving, which can only be satisfied in the Trinity.

This divine truth manifests itself in the New Covenant as in the old—in the Church as in Israel—because, in both, the law is ordered to the liturgy. The law of Israel was ordered to ritual purity. For us today, canon law describes the boundary lines of our home, the Church, the place of sacrifice and sacraments.

In the family, too, we can observe these principles at

work (though here it is difficult to simplify without falling into stereotypes). Traditionally, we identify fatherhood, the masculine principle, with law, logic, and objectivity. Motherhood we associate with love, wisdom, and profound subjective insight. In my own home, where I am father, my objective knowledge sometimes directs me to a course of punishment that I judge to be perfectly logical and just. Kimberly's wisdom and insight, however, often lead me to see that, though I am thinking rightly, my action would fall short of love in this given circumstance with this particular child. I might be right, but I would do wrong unless I submit my knowledge to Kimberly's wisdom. Said Pope Pius XI, "If the man is the head, the woman is the heart, and as he occupies the chief place in ruling, so she may and ought to claim for herself the chief place in love."

Pairing It Down

With the two processions of the Trinity, we have associated a number of complementary pairs of terms:

PROCESSION OF THE SON	PROCESSION OF THE SPIRIT
Knowing	Loving
Intellect	Will
Justification	Sanctification
Husband/Father	Wife/Mother
Legal	Liturgical
Justice	Mercy

Though these terms should be distinguished from one another in thought, they are inseparable in Christian life. Yet, far too often, Christians try to isolate these realities—considering justification apart from sanctification, the law apart from the liturgy, knowing apart from loving. It doesn't work, and the project almost invariably ends by setting inseparable terms in diametric opposition. Their union originates in God, in the "eternal covenant." And what Jesus said of another covenant applies just as well here: "What . . . God has joined together, let not man put asunder" (Mt 19:6).

This theological truth has profound implications for everyday life. What begins in the Trinity, we live out in our unity of life—for persons, for family, for society. Everything God has made—including you and me—bears the image and likeness of the Trinity.

To be fully human, to be fully divinized, then, we need the *whole* Trinity: Father, Son, and Holy Spirit. We need to be justified *and* sanctified; we need the law, *and* we need love. We need to be fathered *and* mothered.

The Hand That Rocks the Credal

It seems almost blasphemous to say this, but Christians *can* place too much emphasis on Christ—if we also neglect the stated purpose of His coming. He came to earth in order to give us the Spirit. He ascended to the Father so that the Spirit could descend on the Church. In these

divine actions, salvation history manifested the divine
processions. The Father sending the Son in history is an
image of the Father generating the Son in eternity. The
descent of the Spirit upon the Church at Pentecost is an
image of the Spirit's procession from the Father and the
Son in eternity.

So if we focus on the works of Christ to the exclusion
of the Holy Spirit, we are missing the most important
work of Christ! The Spirit's essential work is to reproduce Christ's life, suffering, death, and resurrection in
each and all of us. If we neglect the Spirit, we are ne-
glecting Christ, too. "It is to your advantage that I go
away," He told the disciples, "for if I do not go away, the
Counselor will not come to you; but if I go, I will send
Him to you. . . . When the Spirit of truth comes, He
will guide you into all the truth" (Jn 16:7, 13).

When we recite the creed, we must first say, "I believe
in the Holy Spirit," before we can go on to say, "I believe in the holy catholic Church." The sequence is quite
deliberate. For I cannot believe in the Church's truth until I have life in the Spirit. I cannot fully give assent to
Mother Church until I am living the fullness of that life
in the Spirit.

When the Son returned to the Father, He did not leave
us orphans. He sent us the eternal Spirit to live with us
and within us. I firmly believe that we, today, need to
cultivate our devotion to this third Person till the Spirit
is no longer in third place—till the Spirit is, for us, no

longer "the Great Unknown." This will require intensive study, but more intensive prayer. Only then, with our full experience of the two divine processions, will we be fully human, empowered to live out the triunity of God in our everyday lives—knowing and loving, justified and sanctified.

CHAPTER 11

THE SACRED HEARTH

GOD HAS GIVEN us a new family, bound by His New Covenant. What, then, are we to make of our natural families?

Quite simply, we are to make them heaven.

To become all that God has made us to be, we must grow ever more perfectly in His divine image. That means we must give ourselves completely. Now, except in the extraordinary case of martyrdom, we cannot do this all at once—and we can never do it alone. We grow perfect in the image of God only as we "become Christ," in communion with Christ and in communion with others, in communion with the Church.

Three to Get Married

Where does this begin? It begins, ordinarily, in our natural families, which God intends to be the fundamental unit of the Church. The Church and the family are more than "communities"; each is, like the Trinity, a communion of persons. And so they also bear a family resemblance to one another. As the Church is a universal family, the individual family is "the domestic Church" (see CCC, no. 1656).

Through marriage, which is a sacrament of the New Covenant, a household receives a new family resemblance to God. St. Paul wrote, "For this reason I bow my knees before the Father, from Whom every family in heaven and on earth is named" (Eph 3:14–15). Earthly families, then, receive their "name," their identity, their character, from God Himself. They are made in His image.

In the beginning, God created us with the familial imperative. He made us, body and soul, with needs and drives that we could not fulfill by ourselves. He made us so that we would seek completion in another. As St. Augustine wrote, our primordial urge is to "look upon one who looks back in love."

We desire the love of a lover, a spouse, a family—yet those drives leave us only partially fulfilled. I recall sitting in a restaurant with an old friend who told me that he missed the early days of his marriage, when all he and his wife could do was think about one another and lavish romantic attention on one another. In the intervening years, their lives had become cluttered with the normal cares of having children in school, working long hours at the office, and running the household—all necessary and good things. But my friend longed for the loving gaze that never seemed to end.

His is a nostalgia, a longing, that—in God's good providence—can only be fulfilled in the Trinity. Marriage often helps us to see that there is a heaven; indeed, marriage is a profound *sacrament* of the Trinitarian life, the life that is the essence of heaven. Yet marriage itself is not heaven. Indeed, if we place romantic happiness above our true fulfillment in God—if we make "blissful marriage" our ultimate goal—we pervert the meaning of marriage, we blaspheme its sacramental purpose, and we stray down a path that leads us away from heaven.

Now, don't get me wrong. Each spouse *should* try to make the other happy, just as parents *should* strive for the happiness of their children, and children, in turn, *should* wish to please their parents. But we can only find true and lasting happiness in doing God's will; all other pleasures are fleeting. As family members, we only truly "make others happy" when we draw them closer to God, so that they are growing in holiness and living ever more the Trinitarian life of self-giving. We make others happiest when we help them to live in heaven, even here on earth.

Remember, the Hebrew word for "marriage," *kiddushin,* also means "holiness."

Tough Love

Practically speaking, what does all this mean to our family life?

It means that family life on earth gives us constant opportunities to deny ourselves for the sake of others, to give up our comforts and leisure so that others will have comfort and leisure, to look upon others in love even when they look crossly at us. Living this way, we imitate the inner life of God, and we make our homes, our domestic Churches, into sanctuaries of charity, outposts of heaven.

This does not mean that we indulge behavior that is unhealthful or immoral in our family members. Domestic peace never requires the tolerance of sin. On the contrary, we may find many occasions to admonish, correct, and even punish those in our charge. But we will always do so with love, for the good of the other, and never to satisfy our own desire for revenge, power, or control. Reproving someone—when we do it the right way—means showing how that person's behavior is leading him away from true happiness, then helping him to find his way back to the right path.

All of this demands self-sacrifice and self-giving. We must deny the wish to vent the rage that sometimes wells up within us. We must deny ourselves the pleasure of responding with sarcasm or harshness to our siblings, children, spouse, or parents.

$1 + 1 = 1$

Nor does our Trinitarian life stop at the bedroom door. Sexual union is the act that seals and renews the lifelong covenant between a woman and a man. It is the act that makes them a family. It bespeaks a love so strong that "the two become one"—as I said before—a "one" so real that in nine months you might have to give it a name. Sex is an act of extraordinary power, when we let it speak its truth.

Marital love is sacramental. Sex is, in the Church's traditional terms, "*the* marital act," the act that consummates the sacrament of marriage. And a sacrament is a channel of divine grace, which is the very life of God. In sacraments, we incarnate the truth. The word becomes flesh. Thus, for Catholics, sex is a mystery, but it is not something that eludes moral certainty or verifiable reality.

Marital love is sacramental, and the root of the word "sacrament" is *sacramentum,* the Latin word for "oath." When we "make love," we place ourselves under solemn oath—to tell the truth, the whole truth, and nothing but the truth (so help me, God).

And what is the truth we tell under oath? That love makes us one family, like God, Who is three-in-one. Said Pope John Paul II, "God in His deepest mystery is not a solitude, but a family, since He has in Himself fatherhood, sonship, and the essence of the family, which is love."

We tell, too, that God is faithful to His people. Love-making is the metaphor St. Paul chose to apply to Christ and the Church. St. John the Seer, for his part, set forth his visions in the Book of Revelation, which in the original language is "the book of unveiling." An unveiling is the customary climax of a wedding feast, and so is an appropriate way to reveal the marriage supper of Christ and His Church.

All this is the *word* we enflesh in our spousal embrace.

Thus, as an image of God, Who is faithful and Who is one, the family bond between husband and wife must be permanent and indissoluble. Thus, too, as God is fruitful and generous, a married couple must be open to life, willing to cooperate with the Father in the conception of children. This context may help us to understand why the Church forbids acts of contraception, abortion, homosexuality, and adultery—all acts that are contrary to the natural law as well as the supernatural life we share with the Trinity.

Single-Minded

If we were made for the loving gaze, then why must some people remain single? Why on earth would anyone choose celibacy?

Single people are full members of God's family. Indeed, the grace of Christian life gives them a broader vision of family life. In Christ, they are never alone, for they are always among their brothers and sisters in the Communion of Saints. Single Christians walk with close family members wherever they go, at work and at leisure. They are single not because they haven't found a family. They are single as a way of living family life. Their single state enables them to do God's work and to reach people they could not otherwise reach. If their single state isn't vowed and permanent, it's at least providential and present—and it provides them no less an opportunity for total self-giving than married life gives to spouses.

Celibacy—the vowed and permanent single state—is not a repression of the natural. It is, rather, a fulfillment of the natural desires by supernatural means. God made marriage, after all, to be a means to heaven. Yet Jesus says that, in heaven, people "neither marry nor are given in marriage, but are like angels" (Mk 12:25). The celibate chooses to live, right now, as if he or she were already in heaven with God. As Jesus put it, consecrated celibates have "made themselves eunuchs"—that is, they have voluntarily renounced sexual activity—"for the sake of the kingdom of heaven" (Mt 19:12).

For this reason—and for many other, practical reasons—St. Paul passionately argued that celibacy is the more perfect way for Christians to live (see 1 Cor 7). The Book of Revelation corroborates his claim, giving consecrated virgins a prominent place in the life of heaven (14:4).

In sacrificing the pleasures of marriage, the celibate demonstrates the radical quality of his or her self-donation. The celibate priest gives himself completely to God by serving His people. Thus, he begins to live the nuptial bond that will continue in heaven.

The celibacy embraced by the priest and sister makes them more fruitful apostolically. The drive to procreate, joyfully sacrificed, is made sublime and turned into a zeal to win souls for God's covenant family. Jesus Himself promised that this would happen: "Truly, I say to you, there is no man who has left house or wife or brothers or parents or children, for the sake of the kingdom of God, who will not receive manifold more in this time, and in the age to come eternal life" (Lk 18:29–30).

High Fidelity

To look upon one who looks back in love: This was Adam's desire. This was my desire (though I didn't know it) the day I met Kimberly Kirk. Yet finding Miss Right was not the end of the story for Adam, or for me, or for any other man. Waking up to Mr. Right was not the end of the story for Eve, or for Kimberly, or for any other woman.

Adam had to *prove* his love—and we all have to prove our love, each and every day. I don't mean that he had to satisfy Eve's insecurities. He had, rather, to give himself completely for her sake. To do so would be to live as God lives, and that would have been his entry to divine life.

Anything less than total sacrifice would have been less than love. In love, we must give our *all*. Think about it in these terms: A woman says to her husband, "Tell me the truth, honey—have you been faithful to me?" Can a man honestly answer yes if he's been faithful ninety-nine percent of the time? Could he still say he was true to her, since his faithful days far outnumbered his adulterous days?

No way. Marriage is an all-or-nothing proposition. We can't hold anything back. And that is yet another way marriage serves as a sacrament, a revelation, of the love of God. For His covenant is a nuptial bond requiring total fidelity. It's the truth and nothing but the truth. It's the fullness of God's life, leaving no room for sin or doubt.

It will demand our total self-giving. Like Adam, we will be tested—not because God is some supernatural sadist who likes to watch us fail, but because otherwise we could not freely choose to live and love as He does.

Going on Vocation

Appropriately enough, we can discern *three* stages in our Christian life: vocation, probation, and oblation—God's call, our response, and our offering. These are not once-and-done stages. Rather, they recur in various ways as we mature. Christian life proceeds, like this book, with frequent returns to our beginnings, only to build toward fulfillment.

Vocation. The first stage corresponds to self-identification. God the Father calls us, and so we know we are His children. In faith, we accept our sonship.

Like any good father, God loves His children, but He loves us too much to let us remain children forever. He wants us to grow into a full maturity, to live as He lives. We cannot do this without . . .

156

Probation. This second stage corresponds to our self-mastery in imitation of the Son of God, Jesus Christ. We have to prove our love by choosing to love in a divine way, by choosing to give ourselves totally. Yet we cannot offer to God what we have not first conquered. We cannot give away what we do not first possess.

Think, for a moment, about the ancient Israelites. Imagine the high priest trying to bring to the altar a large and rambunctious goat—or even a small bull! He could not sacrifice the animal until he had subdued it, bound it, brought it under control. Well, neither can we give ourselves away until we have taken possession of ourselves.

To take another example from ancient history: The Israelites could not enter the Promised Land until they subdued seven peoples who lived there. St. Gregory the Great pointed out that this is a literal historical fact that corresponds to a deep spiritual truth. We need to conquer the seven deadly sins—wrath, lust, greed, gluttony, sloth, envy, and pride—before we can enter the Promised Land of Trinitarian life.

This is our testing, our proving, our probation. It requires effort and a certain degree of suffering. More, it demands fortitude grounded in hope. But if we persevere, our testing will culminate in our . . .

Oblation. The final stage marks our self-sacrifice, when we have renounced ourselves completely for the sake of another, specifically for God. This is when we become what we were made to become, when we fulfill our created purpose, when we shine forth the divine image. In the end, we possess ourselves in order to give ourselves away, so that we can become ourselves. There is no other way to live in Christ, for this is the way Christ lives. We can make our offering only through our participation in the Holy Spirit, Who perfects our love.

Vocation, probation, oblation. Faith, hope, and love. Father, Son, and Spirit. Our ultimate goods—our way, our truth, and our life—do seem to come in threes.

CHAPTER 12

A Sure Thing

I BEGAN THIS BOOK with a reflection on falling in love, marrying, and having a child. Though I've been blessed to study under some of the great minds and souls of the Christian world, nothing has helped me to grow, as a Christian and as a theologian, so much as these exalted family moments. Rightly does the Church call marriage a sacrament, for a sacrament is, by definition, an outward sign of inner grace—and grace is a sharing in the life of God.

Heirborn

Return with me to the story of the birth of my first child, my son Michael. After the cesarean birth and a brief hospital stay for recovery, Kimberly and Michael came home to me. Kimberly had been transformed by the experience. The surgery had left her scarred, exhausted, and temporarily stooped; yet never had she looked so beautiful—and never had the aura of God's Spirit glowed more gloriously for me than when I watched Kimberly get up night after night. After thirty hours of hard labor, then major surgery, Kimberly had come home to long nights of fitful sleep interrupted by feedings and burpings. I needed only to open my eyes and I could *see* self-giving and life-giving love.

I watched in awe as she fed my son from her breast. My mind rang with passages from the Scriptures:

"But I have calmed and quieted my soul, like a child quieted at its mother's breast" (Ps 131:2).

"Rejoice with Jerusalem, and be glad for her, all you who love her . . . that you may suck and be satisfied with her consoling breasts" (Is 66:10–11).

My wife could say, with Our Lord, "This is my body, given for you." In her own body, Kimberly was extending the mystery of the New Covenant. As Our Lord feeds the Church, so she fed our child—from her own substance.

Words Cannot Describe

I was amazed by her sacrifice. Yet I also wanted to help, to relieve her burdens. One night around three A.M., after Kimberly had been nursing Michael for a half hour, I felt inspired to ask if I might take the baby for a while. She agreed, smiling with relief and gratitude. I took

Michael in my arms, and Kimberly carefully positioned herself for sleep.

I walked into the next room, patting Michael lightly on the back, trying to draw out a burp so that he could sleep comfortably again. I was almost teary-eyed with love for this boy—my son, my likeness, my heir. I held him close and patted him as I had seen Kimberly pat him. But perhaps I went about the job a little too vigorously because, suddenly, I heard an abrupt hiccup, and I was overcome by a certain warmth.

Something warm and wet was running down my back.

Now, this was the first time anyone had ever vomited on me. And I wasn't sure how to react. So I lifted my son up from my shoulder and cradled him in my arms, and I looked into the bright, sparkling, wide-awake eyes of this little person—the only person who had ever thrown up on me.

If you'd asked me, a year before, how I would feel looking into the eyes of someone who'd just vomited on me, I would have been repulsed. But as I looked down at this boy, all the love in the world was welling up inside me. Though I'd known the love of my parents, and I knew the love of my wife, I had never felt this way before.

I didn't *need* to hold him anymore. Now that he'd gotten that out of his system, he would have easily gone back to sleep. But instead of putting him down, I sat on the rocking chair, and, in the soft moonlight, I looked into those eyes for . . . I don't know how long. I had thought Kimberly was the be-all and end-all of love. Now I felt our mutual love multiplied exponentially.

I was looking at Michael, and the clearest words came to my heart: *You see how much you love him?*

"Yes, Lord! Words can't describe!"

Well, you can't possibly love your child more than I love My children.

That realization quite suddenly took my breath away.

The month before or the day before, I could have told you the substance of that statement as an obvious theological fact: God is infinite and eternal, and so He has an infinite capacity for love; I, however, am finite and mortal; therefore, God can love far more than I can.

But what I was experiencing that night at three A.M. wasn't a theological argument or a doctrinal formula. It was a love message, delivered personally, though without an audible voice or a whisper.

For the better part of an hour, I just rocked in my chair, holding my baby close to me and basking in the thought that I loved this boy more than I could say—and yet my Father God loved me even more!

Without a Doubt

Now I have a confession to make. I've had many *confessions* to make!

Though with the birth of each of my six children I've grown in that luminous insight—and in the afterglow of my sonship—I've also lost the glow, many, many times. I'm a sinner, and sin takes away the glow from our lives as children of God. For, when we sin, we no longer look to God as Father. "Original sin is not only the violation of a positive command of God," said Pope John Paul II. "Original sin attempts . . . to abolish fatherhood, destroying its rays which permeate the created world, placing in doubt the truth about God Who is Love and leaving man only with a sense of the master-slave relationship. . . . the enslaved man is driven to take sides against the Master who kept him enslaved."

When I sin, I lose sight of God's fatherhood, and I find myself begging Him to show me again what He showed me that night when I held Michael. "How do I move from the theoretical certitude of divine love to the practical assurance that I'm Your child?"

Whenever this mood comes upon me, the Holy Spirit prompts me to ask myself a question: Well, how do the Hahn children know that they're Scott's kids?

They have a number of rock-solid reasons for assurance.

They live in my house. Whenever they say they're "going home," they mean that they're going to the old house on Belleview Boulevard, the house whose lease bears my name, the house on which I pay taxes.

They're called by my name. Each one, from great to

small, is a "Hahn kid." It's my family name that's posted on the front door. Whenever they sign on the dotted line, they end with four letters they received from my ancestors: *H-a-h-n*.

They sit at my table. They're sure to remember this one, because they sure like to eat. I like it, too, when we all eat together.

They share my flesh and blood. They can thank me for it, or scowl at me for it, but they've all got it in one form or another: the family resemblance. If they can't see it in the family portrait, they can find it in a DNA test. They're chips off the Hahn block.

My bride is their mother. And I remind them, whenever I can, that they owe me big-time, because I got them the best of moms.

We're always celebrating together. The family is, by nature, a memory-making machine. We Hahns celebrate birthdays, anniversaries, name days, feast days, holidays. Pile on the desserts. Light the candles. Get ready to sing. To be a Hahn is to celebrate continuously.

They receive instruction and discipline from me. I don't discipline the neighbor kids, or the kids in the next booth at McDonald's. So the kids I discipline know that they're mine. And discipline is not just instruction; it's spending time together, modeling virtues, teaching them to reason by the way we carry on a conversation. Discipline is the way we make disciple-ing.

On these grounds (and more), my children need never

wonder, "What am I doing in this place?" or "Will they feed me?" They know they belong in the House of Hahn.

Marks of the Church

Has our heavenly Father given us any less in the Catholic Church? Think of the same seven assurances my children have, now applied to you and me as members of the Church.

We live in His house. As members of the Catholic Church, we live in the house Christ promised to build—as a wise man does—upon the rock (Mt 16:17–19). In the Greek New Testament, the metaphor most often applied to the Church is the "household of God." "Christ was faithful over God's house as a son. And we are His house if we hold fast our confidence and pride in our hope" (Heb 3:6). "So then you are no longer strangers and sojourners, but you are fellow citizens with the saints and *members of the household of God,* built upon the foundation of the apostles and prophets, Christ Jesus Himself being the cornerstone" (Eph 2:19–20).

We are called by His name. In baptism, we are marked for life in the name of the Father, Son, and Holy Spirit (Mt 28:18–20). Thus, we "were sealed with the promised Holy Spirit, which is the guarantee of our inheritance until we acquire possession of it" (Eph 1:13–14). Our family unity is thus based upon "the unity of the

Spirit in the bond of peace. There is one body and one Spirit, just as you were called to the one hope that belongs to your call, one Lord, one faith, one baptism, one God and Father of us all" (Eph 4:3–6).

We sit at His table. We "partake of the table of the Lord" (1 Cor 10:21)—as God's children—in the Eucharist, which Jesus instituted with His disciples "as they were at table eating" (Mk 14:18).

We share in His flesh and blood. In Holy Communion, we come to share in Christ's flesh and blood, according to His command: "Truly, truly, I say to you, unless you eat the flesh of the Son of Man and drink His blood, you have no life in you; he who eats My flesh and drinks My blood has eternal life, and I will raise him up at the last day. For My flesh is food indeed, and My blood is drink indeed. He who eats My flesh and drinks My blood abides in Me, and I in him" (Jn 6:53–56).

His bride is our mother. The Church is Christ's Bride, the heavenly Jerusalem (Eph 5:21–32; Rv 21:1–10, 22–23), and also our mother. "But the Jerusalem above is free, and she is our mother" (Gal 4:26). Even more, Jesus gave us His mother, the Virgin Mary, to be our mother. "When Jesus saw His mother, and the disciple whom He loved standing near, He said to His mother, 'Woman, behold your son!' Then He said to the disciple, 'Behold, your mother!' And from that hour the disciple took her to his own home" (Jn 19:26–27).

We celebrate as a family. We gather together as the children of God to celebrate, most especially in the eucharistic banquet. "Christ, our paschal lamb, has been sacrificed. Let us, therefore, celebrate the festival" (1 Cor 5:7–8). For this reason, God calls us to "be filled with the Spirit, addressing one another in psalms and hymns and spiritual songs, singing and making melody to the Lord with all your heart" (Eph 5:18–19). As Catholics, we celebrate different feast days to honor our Blessed Mother and our spiritual brothers and sisters, the saints—not only for their holy lives but also for their glorious deaths, which thus became a heavenly home-coming.

We receive instruction and discipline from Him. We receive guidance from God's revelation, through Scripture, Tradition, and the Church's teaching authority. We accept penance and seek reconciliation through the sacraments. We look to others in the Church who have the "grace of state" to instruct us in Christ's name, from the local bishop to our personal confessor. Our heavenly Father even uses our labors and sufferings to teach and guide us.

"My son, do not regard lightly the discipline of the Lord, nor lose courage when you are punished by Him. For the Lord disciplines him whom He loves, and chastises every son whom He receives. It is for discipline that you have to endure. God is treating you as sons; for what son is there whom his father does not discipline? . . . For they disciplined us for a short time at their pleasure, but He disciplines us for our good, that we may share His holiness" (Heb 12:5–7, 10).

The Assurance of Things Hoped For

All this is only the beginning. We need not search far for other reassurances. Take, for example, the hope we have by God's grace. "Now faith is the assurance of things hoped for," says Heb 11:1. Yet I believe that hope is the most neglected of the three theological virtues. Many Catholics find themselves burdened with a faith that is devoid of hope. Often, they disdain hope because they have wrong ideas about what it is. Perhaps they've confused it with mere "wishful thinking"—"I hope I win the lottery! I hope my team wins the World Series."

Some hopes are unlikely, and some are impossible. But some hopes are quite reasonable. When I hope to see my friend Dan, who lives across the country, I call my travel agent. I get on a plane owned by a reputable airline, steered by a trained pilot. And I have good grounds to hope that I'll see my friend.

In faith, we have *more* assurance, and *more realistic* assurance, that we'll get what we hope for—more reasons than I have when I step on that plane. We have God's oath. Look closely at this remarkable passage from Hebrews:

169

For when God made a promise to Abraham, since He had no one greater by whom to swear, He swore by Himself. . . . Men indeed swear by a greater than themselves, and in all their disputes an oath is final for confirmation. So when God desired to show more convincingly to the heirs of the promise the unchangeable character of His purpose, He interposed with an oath. . . . We have this as a sure and steadfast anchor of the soul, a hope that enters into the inner shrine behind the curtain, where Jesus has gone as a forerunner on our behalf. (6:13, 16–17, 19–20)

"Yeah, that's all well and good," you might say, "but God only swears oaths to great patriarchs like Abraham, right? What's in this for me?"

It's all in there for you, because God has sworn an oath to you. Remember, the Latin word for "oath" is *sacramentum*—"sacrament." God has given you oath after oath, sacrament after sacrament, so that you'd never be afraid, never be anxious, never doubt His fatherly care. He's given you His own seven reasons, sacramental reasons, for assurance: baptism, confirmation, confession, Holy Communion, marriage, holy orders, and the anointing of the sick.

Home Free

If you're anything like me, you find it much easier to think and talk about being a child of God than to believe it from the heart—and live it. Nowhere is the struggle greater—or more vital to our spiritual well-being—than the issue of personal assurance. In other words, how can we be fully assured that God loves us as His children?

The promise of salvation is what all Christians share: Catholic, Orthodox, and Protestant. Jesus died for our sins. If you believe that, you'll be saved. It's a promise. But the assurance of hope comes only with the oath. As Catholics, we have the Gospel and the sacraments—both the promise and the oath. And if that's not reassuring, nothing ever can be.

Our heavenly Father has given to us rock-solid grounds for assurance, more than any earthly father (even in the House of Hahn) has ever provided. Not only can we know that we are God's children, but we can be confident that our omnipotent Father will get us home safely. "I am sure that He who began a good work in you will bring it to completion at the day of Jesus Christ" (Phil 1:6).

Of course, assurance does not mean that our lives will be free of struggle and suffering or that we can relax and take it easy. Nor does it mean that, since God is our Father and Christ our brother, we can begin to take the Trinity for granted the way we, perhaps, have taken our earthly families for granted.

With our divinization comes not a lower standard for struggle, but a much higher standard. For fathers expect more from children than judges expect from defendants, or bosses from employees, or teachers from students. Indeed, the standard is so high as to seem impossible to us.

Yet Christ's word comes to us as it came to His disciples, when they first faced the enormity of the task. "Jesus looked at them and said to them, 'With men this is impossible, but with God all things are possible'" (Mt 19:26).

That's why we say we believe in God the "Father almighty." Fatherly omnipotence alone makes it possible for us to enjoy the "fatherhood of God and brotherhood of man," on earth and in heaven.

No good father demands of his children more than he himself has given. God asks us to "be perfect," but only because He has given us divine life to make it possible. The command is inseparable from the gift, and the gift is inseparable from the command. For our part, we can do no better than to respond in loving obedience to the God who has lavished life upon us.

What we can't do God can, and He has done it. Adam and Eve, and Scott and Kimberly—and you!—can live as the image and likeness of God, as the children of God, because God has willed it to be so.

SOURCES AND REFERENCES

Page 6: "It is not good that the man should be alone." See the discussion of "original solitude" in Pope John Paul II, *The Original Unity of Man and Woman* (Boston: St. Paul Books and Media, 1981), pp. 43–49.

Page 11: ". . . a key to understanding what we find inscrutable: the Trinity." See Pope John Paul II, "Holy Trinity: Model for All Families," *L'Osservatore Romano*, June 10, 1998, p. 1: "In the Trinity we can discern the primordial model of the human family, consisting of a man and woman called to give themselves to each other in a communion of love that is open to life. In the Trinity we also find the model of the ecclesial family, in which all Christians are called to live in a relationship of real sharing and solidarity."

Page 16: "What does the Bible mean by family?" See L. Perdue et al., *Families in Ancient Israel* (Louisville, Ky.:

Westminster John Knox Press, 1997); C. Osiek and D. Balch, *Families in the New Testament World* (Louisville, Ky.: Westminster John Knox Press, 1997). For an insightful treatment of the biblical view of the family as a corporate personality, see J. de Fraine, S.J., *Adam and the Family of Man* (Staten Island, N.Y.: Alba House, 1965).

Page 17: "The Tribal Belt." On the religious nature of patriarchal family cultures in antiquity, see K. van der Toorn, *Family Religion in Babylonia, Syria and Israel* (Leiden: Brill, 1995); C. Pressler, *The View of Women Found in the Deuteronomic Family Laws* (New York: Walter de Gruyter, 1993); C. Dawson, "The Patriarchal Family in History," in *Dynamics of World History* (London: Sheed and Ward, 1957), pp. 156–66. On the disputed "tribal origins" of ancient Israel in Scripture, see A. Malamat, *History of Biblical Israel* (Leiden: Brill, 2001); W. G. Dever, *What Did the Biblical Writers Know and When Did They Know It?* (Grand Rapids, Mich.: Eerdmans, 2001); T. L. Thompson, *The Mythic Past* (New York: Basic Books, 1998); K. L. Sparks, *Ethnicity and Identity in Ancient Israel* (Winona Lake, Ind.: Eisenbrauns, 1998).

Page 19: "Ancestors were revered in ancient cultures." F. de Coulanges, *The Ancient City* (Garden City, N.Y.: Doubleday, 1956), p. 40; H. Maine, *Ancient Law* (New York: Dutton, 1977); E. Schillebeeckx, *Marriage: Human Reality and Saving Mystery* (New York: Sheed and Ward,

1965), p. 234: "Each family had its own domestic liturgy. . . . Its priest was the *paterfamilias* of the domestic hearth. . . . The ancient family was thus, by definition, a religious community."

Page 19: "Priesthood was passed from father to son . . ." H. C. Brichto, "Kin, Cult, Land and Afterlife: A Biblical Complex," *Hebrew Union College Annual* 44 (1979): 1–54: "There is ample evidence that the role of priest in the Israelite family had at one time been filled by the firstborn" (p. 46). See G. N. Knoppers, "The Preferential Status of the Eldest Son Revoked?" in S. L. McKenzie and T. Romer, eds., *Rethinking the Foundations* (Berlin: Walter de Gruyter, 2000), pp. 115–26; B. J. Beitzel, "The Right of the Firstborn in the Old Testament," in W. C. Kaiser and R. F. Youngblood, eds., *Essays on the Old Testament* (Chicago: Moody, 1986), pp. 179–95; I. Mendelsohn, "On the Preferential Status of the Eldest Son," *Bulletin of the American Society of Oriental Research* 156 (1959): 38–40. For a similar outlook in patristic and medieval sources, see St. Jerome *MPL* 23:980, and St. Thomas Aquinas *Summa theologica* II–II, Q. 87, art. 1.

Page 20: "Covenant was an ancient family's way . . ." See F. M. Cross, "Kinship and Covenant in Ancient Israel," in *From Epic to Canon* (Baltimore: Johns Hopkins University Press, 1998), pp. 3–21: "The language of covenant, kinship-in-law, is taken from the language of kinship, kinship-in-flesh" (p. 11). It should be noted that covenants could also be made between those already related by kin (e.g., David and Jonathan in 1 Sm 20:12–17; the Israelite elders and David in 2 Sm 5:1–3). Covenants thus served not only to initiate and extend family relations and obligations but to renew/reinforce natural kinship bonds; cf. G. P. Hugenberger, *Marriage as a Covenant* (Leiden: Brill, 1994), pp. 177–215. Also see C. Baker, *Covenant and Liberation* (New York: Peter Lang, 1991), p. 38: "We may take as our working description of covenant . . . a solemn and externally manifested commitment which strengthens kinship and family concern between both parties."

Page 21: "the covenant between Israel and Yahweh . . ." D. J. McCarthy, S.J., "Israel My Firstborn Son," *Way* 5 (1965): 186; see idem, *Treaty and Covenant*, 2nd ed. (Rome: Pontifical Biblical Institute, 1981); P. Kalluveetitil, *Declaration and Covenant* (Rome: Pontifical Biblical Institute, 1982), p. 212; Cross, "Kinship and Covenant," pp. 12–13: "The league was also a kinship organization, a covenant of families and tribes. . . . The league in ideal form was conceived as twelve tribes, related at once by covenant and kinship. . . . Israel is the kindred (*'am*) of Yahweh. . . . This formula must be understood as legal language, the language of kinship-in-law, or in other words, the language of covenant."

Page 21: "In his monumental work . . ." C. C. Zimmerman, *Family and Civilization* (New York: Harper and Brothers, 1947), pp. 128–29.

Page 22: "There are many remarkable differences in these historical stages." See Zimmerman, *Family and Civilization,* pp. 120–210. Zimmerman introduces his "new classification" in terms of the following questions: "Of the total power in the society, how much belongs to the family? Of the total amount of control of action in the society, how much is left for the family? What role does the family play in the total business of society? These are the real problems. If we want to marry or to break up a family, whom do we consult, the family, the church, or the state?" (p. 125). Zimmerman describes the essentially religious nature of the trustee family: "Among the early Romans, the religious conceptions were household and familistic. The people were bound together by a feeling of sacredness" (p. 146). "There were social restrictions—the religious convictions of the family and the people and the family council. . . . The same domestication of religion was prevalent among the early Greeks. As a matter of fact, it seems true of all early civilized groups. . . . it is the thesis of the Vedic Hymns and other ancient Hindu documents. Confucianism itself is founded upon the development of the domestic religion of the early Chinese. . . . This was also true for the early Romans. . . . However, race does not seem to be the factor, since all great civilized peoples have corresponding religions. This domestication of religion was the fact which makes the ordinary conception of the husband as the owner of wife and children, with the power to purchase and sell them, entirely erroneous. Religion creates a unity, something which has no market value. Husband and wife (as well as parent and child) were bound by ties a thousand times more meaningful than market price" (pp. 147–48). Zimmerman then illustrates this by tracing the periodic evolution of marriage from the trustee (as sacrament), through the domestic (as concubinage), to the atomistic (as mere *"copula carnalis* for pleasure") (pp. 148–53). "Thus, in the trustee period, adultery, along with one or two other crimes, is the infamous act against the whole society (kinship group which connects the person with life)" (p. 153). This is reminiscent of the ancient Israelite laws against adultery (Ex 20:14), for which capital punishment was prescribed (Lv 20:10; Dt 22:22).

Besides Zimmerman, I have greatly profited from other more recent family studies, including J. D. Schloen, *The House of the Father as Fact and Symbol: Patrimonialism in Ugarit and the Ancient Near East* (Cambridge, Mass.: Harvard University Press, 2001); P. Riley, *Civilizing Sex: On Chastity and the Common Good* (Edinburgh: T. & T. Clark, 2000); C. R. Jones, *Kinship Diplomacy in the Ancient World* (Cambridge, Mass.: Harvard University Press, 1999); A. Burguiere et al., eds., *A History of the Family,* 2 vols. (Cambridge, Mass.: Harvard University

Press, 1996); B. Gottlieb, *The Family in the Western World* (New York: Oxford University Press, 1993); A. D. Smith, *The Ethnic Origins of Nations* (New York: Basil Blackwell, 1986); P. Abbott, *The Family on Trial: Special Relationships in Modern Political Thought* (University Park, Pa.: Pennsylvania State University Press, 1981); J.-L. Flandrin, *Families in Former Times* (New York: Cambridge University Press, 1979); A. Moret and G. Davy, *From Tribe to Empire: Social Organization Among Primitives and in the Ancient East* (London: Routledge and Kegan Paul; New York: Cooper Square, 1970); W. J. Goode, *World Revolution and Family Patterns* (New York: Free Press, 1963).

Page 25: "The First Christian Revolution." See J. Hellerman, *The Church as Family: Early Christian Communities as Surrogate Kin Groups* (Ph.D. diss., University of California, Los Angeles; Ann Arbor, Mich.: University Microfilms, 1998), p. 6; idem, *The Ancient Church as Family* (Minneapolis: Fortress Press, 2001). On the pervasiveness of New Testament family terms and images, see K. O. Sandnes, *A New Family: Conversion and Ecclesiology in the Early Church with Cross-Cultural Comparisons* (New York: Peter Lang, 1994), pp. 64–82, and R. Banks, *Paul's Idea of Community: The Early House Churches in Their Historical Setting* (Grand Rapids, Mich.: Eerdmans, 1980), p. 53: "So numerous are these [family terms], and so frequently do they appear, that the comparison of the Christian community with a 'family' must be regarded as the most significant metaphorical usage of all."

Page 27: "God, to Jesus Christ, is 'Abba,'—which means 'Daddy' . . ." This is repeatedly echoed in the catechetical teaching of Pope John Paul II, especially in his Wednesday audiences (e.g., March 3, 1999; March 10, 1999; January 5, 2000). On the Church's formal recognition at Nicea of the reality of Christ's divine sonship as metaphysical ("the same substance"), and not metaphorical ("a similar substance"), see J. Ratzinger, *Behold the Pierced One: An Approach to a Spiritual Christology* (San Francisco: Ignatius Press, 1986), pp. 32–37.

Page 32: "This new conception must have seemed subversive." The "subversive" effects of Jesus' subordinating natural human kinship to supernatural divine ties of the Spirit are treated in S. Oporto, "Kingdom and Family in Conflict," in J. J. Pilch, ed., *Social Scientific Models for Interpreting the Bible* (Leiden: Brill, 2001), pp. 210–38; H. Moxnes, ed., *Constructing Early Christian Families: Family as Social Reality and Metaphor* (New York: Routledge, 1997); D. Jacobs-Malina, *Beyond Patriarchy: The Images of Family in Jesus* (New York: Paulist Press, 1993). This subordination was reinterpreted by patristic figures in ecclesial, sacramental, and ascetical terms; see E. A. Clark, *Reading Renunciation: Asceticism and Scripture in Early Christianity* (Princeton, N.J.: Princeton University Press, 1999), especially pp. 177–203.

Page 34: "Sociologist Rodney Stark . . ." R. Stark, *The Rise of Christianity* (San Francisco: HarperCollins, 1997), p. 59. Also see J. G. van der Watt, *Family of the King* (Leiden: Brill, 2000); G. Nathan, *The Family in Late Antiquity: The Rise of Christianity and the Endurance of Tradition* (New York: Routledge, 2000).

Page 35: "Into this milieu, Christianity arrived . . ." "A Double Take on Early Christianity: An Interview with Rodney Stark," *Touchstone,* January–February 2000, p. 44.

Page 42: "God's Family Properties." Some material here is adapted from S. Hahn, "The Mystery of the Family of God," in S. Hahn and L. Suprenant, eds., *Catholic for a Reason* (Steubenville, Ohio: Emmaus Road, 1998), pp. 5–9.

Page 42: "In the light of the New Testament . . ." Pope John Paul II, *Letter to Families* (Boston: St. Paul Books and Media, 1994), p. 14.

Page 42: "God in His deepest mystery is not a solitude . . ." Pope John Paul II, *Puebla: A Pilgrimage of Faith* (Boston: Daughters of St. Paul, 1979), p. 86. See B. de

Margerie, S.J., *The Christian Trinity in History* (Still River, Mass.: St. Bede's Publications, 1982), p. xix: "The directive idea, underlying our Trinitarian analysis and synthesis, is this: in the created world the total, though not adequate nor still less exhaustive, image of the Trinitarian mystery is man, personal and familial."

Page 42: "The divine 'We' . . ." Pope John Paul II, *Letter to Families,* pp. 13–14.

Page 43: "The Trinity is God's personal identity . . ." See R. Nicole, "The Wisdom of Marriage," in J. I. Packer and S. K. Soderlund, eds., *The Way of Wisdom* (Grand Rapids, Mich.: Zondervan, 2000), pp. 281–82: "This Trinitarian unity is an eternal fact: God is, was, and always will be the Three-in-One, and there only ever has been, or will be, one single divine purpose that embraces everything."

Page 45: "The divine mystery of the Incarnation . . ." Pope John Paul II, *Letter to Families,* p. 7.

Page 45: "Whereas Adam and Eve . . ." See Pope John Paul II, *Redemptoris Custos* (On the Person and Mission of Saint Joseph in the Life of Christ and of the Church) (Boston: St. Paul Books and Media, 1989), p. 14.

Page 46: "so admirably reflects the life of communion . . ." The spontaneous remarks of Pope John Paul II to the children of Holy Family of Nazareth Parish (February 9, 1992) are quoted by J. F. Chorpenning, O.S.F.S., "John Paul II's Theology of the Mystery of the Holy Family," *Communio* 28 (2001): 140–66 (163).

Page 47: "communion of persons" Pope John Paul II, *Letter to Families*, pp. 6, 7.

Page 47: "Human marriage is a living, embodied analogy . . ." See P. J. Miller, F.S.E., *Marriage: The Sacrament of Divine-Human Communion* (Quincy, Ill.: Franciscan Press, 1996).

Page 51: "Nature's seeming preference for threeness . . ." N. R. Wood, *The Secret of the Universe: God, Man, and Matter* (Grand Rapids, Mich.: Eerdmans, 1955).

Page 54: "The answer lies in the details of Adam's creation." On the link between the seventh day (sabbath), the covenant, and oath-swearing, see S. R. Hirsch, *Jewish Symbolism* (New York: Feldheim Publishers, 1995), pp. 97–105; A. J. Heschel, *The Sabbath* (New York: Farrar, Straus and Young, 1951), pp. 29–67; S. Hahn, *A Father Who Keeps His Promises: God's Covenant Love* (Ann Arbor, Mich.: Servant, 1998), pp. 49–53; idem, "Kinship by Covenant: A Biblical Theological Study of Covenant Types and Texts in the Old and New Testaments" (Ph.D. diss., Marquette University; Ann Arbor, Mich.:

University Microfilms, 1995), pp. 66–73; R. Murray, S.J., *The Cosmic Covenant* (London: Sheed and Ward, 1992), pp. 2–13; N.-E. A. Andreasen, *The Old Testament Sabbath: A Tradition-Historical Investigation* (Missoula, Mont.: Society of Biblical Literature, 1972), p. 7; R. de Vaux, O.P., *Ancient Israel: Its Life and Institutions,* vol. 2 (New York: McGraw-Hill, 1961), p. 481: "The 'sign' of the Covenant made at the dawn of creation is the observance of the sabbath by man (cf. Ez 20:12, 20)." See Gn 21:27–32; Ez 17:13–19; Wis 18:6–22; Lk 1:73.

Page 62: "God had given the primal couple . . ." See Vatican II, *Gaudium et Spes* 18, which refers to that "bodily death from which man would have been immune had he not sinned."

Page 63: "Making Sense of the Story." Regarding the Genesis narrative, the *Catechism of the Catholic Church* says, "The account of the fall in Genesis 3 uses figurative language, but affirms a primeval event, a deed that took place *at the beginning of the history of man.* Revelation gives us the certainty of faith that the whole of human history is marked by the original fault freely committed by our first parents" (no. 390; italics in the original). "With the progress of Revelation, the reality of sin is also illuminated. Although to some extent the People of God in the Old Testament had tried to understand the pathos of the human condition in the light of the history of the fall

narrated in Genesis, they could not grasp this story's ultimate meaning, which is revealed only in the light of the
death and Resurrection of Jesus Christ. We must know
Christ as the source of grace in order to know Adam as
the source of sin" (no. 388). Still, the question remains,
what literary genre is employed to affirm this "event" in
such figurative language? See L. Alonso-Schokel, S.J.,
"Sapiential and Covenant Themes in Genesis 2–3," in
D. J. McCarthy and W. B. Callen, eds., *Modern Biblical
Studies* (Milwaukee: Bruce, 1967), pp. 49–61; G. E.
Mendenhall, "The Shady Side of Wisdom," in H. N.
Bream et al., eds., *Old Testament Studies* (Philadelphia:
Temple University Press, 1974), pp. 319–34. Mendenhall
shows how "the apparently naïve and childlike story is
actually a work of utmost artistry and sophistication that
stems from the 'wisdom' tradition of ancient Israel. It is
a *mashal:* an 'analogy.' . . . Like the book of Job, which it
closely resembles . . . it stems from a wisdom tradition
that had been chastened by calamity" (p. 320). The term
mashal admits of a wide range of possible translations
(e.g., "proverb," "byword," "riddle," "parable"). Mendenhall goes on to explain how it applies to Gn 2–3: "A
mashal may serve as a ground, precedent, or justification
of existing reality—similar to the category of myth in ancient pagan cultures. Historical persons and events become *mashal* also, as for example in Deut 28:37" (pp.
326–27): "You [Israel] shall become a horror, a proverb
[mashal] . . . among all the peoples where the Lord will

lead you away." The term is frequently applied in many other contexts where God's plan is to use the catastrophic results of Israel's sin as instruction and warning to the Gentiles (1 Kgs 9:7; Ps 44:14; Jer 24:9; Ez 14:8). A similar application can be made with the narrative of Adam's fall. Also noteworthy is how *mashal* can denote a "riddle," particularly with a test of wisdom in an ordeal situation (see Samson's riddle in Jgs 14:14). Such riddles quite often occur in marital contexts like Samson's, and typically depend on double meanings, where the surface meaning masks a deeper and truer meaning (e.g., the Babylonian riddle: How is she fat without eating?). This literary form serves to conceal even as it reveals, thereby beckoning readers to probe more thoughtfully for deeper insight. It is this kind of literary usage that I see here in Gn 2–3 (a riddle used as a test of wisdom in an ordeal situation). Double meanings hover about all the key terms: life, death, wise, trees. Thus, like Adam, we must discern between the human and divine forms of life, death, and wisdom—as they are signified by the two trees (cf. Prv 3:18 and 11:30; divine Wisdom is the tree of life bearing fruit for righteous persons who fear the Lord more than they fear suffering).

Page 65: "The death of the man is the separation . . ." Philo *Legum allegoriae* 1.105–8, as cited by M. Kolarcik, *The Ambiguity of Death in the Book of Wisdom 1–6* (Rome: Pontifical Biblical Institute, 1991), p. 77. See the insightful discussion of M. Fishbane, *The Kiss of God: Spiritual and Mystical Death in Judaism* (Seattle: University of Washington Press, 1994).

Page 68: "What is clear is that Adam faced a life-threatening force . . ." A fuller treatment of this interpretive approach to the temptation narrative may be found in Hahn, *A Father Who Keeps His Promises,* pp. 57–76; for references to ancient and modern Jewish and Christian sources, see pp. 272–76. The identification of the serpent of the Fall with Satan, as a deadly dragon, is explicit in New Testament texts; see Rv 12:9: "The great dragon was thrown down, that ancient serpent, who is called the Devil and Satan" (also Rv 20:2). For ancient Near Eastern, intertestamental, and rabbinic parallels, see *Life of Adam and Eve* 9–13, 37–39; *3 Apoc. of Baruch* 4:1–5:3; *Test. of Asher* 7:3; *Test. of Solomon* 6, 12; *Apoc. of Abraham* 23:1–12; *1 Enoch* 60:1–8; C. Grottanelli, "The Enemy King Is a Monster," in *Kings and Prophets* (New York: Oxford University Press, 1999), pp. 47–72; M. Fishbane, "The Great Dragon Battle and Talmudic Redaction," in *The Exegetical Imagination* (Cambridge, Mass.: Harvard University Press, 1998), pp. 41–54; G. A. Boyd, "Slaying Leviathan: Cosmic Warfare and the Preservation and Restoration of Creation," in *God at War* (Downers Grove, Ill.: InterVarsity Press, 1997), pp. 93–113; B. F. Batto, *Slaying the Dragon* (Louisville, Ky.: Westminster John Knox Press, 1992); J. Day, *God's Conflict with the*

Dragon and the Sea (New York: Oxford University Press, 1988); N. Forsyth, *The Old Enemy: Satan and the Combat Myth* (Princeton, N.J.: Princeton University Press, 1987); C. Kloos, *Yhwh's Combat with the Sea* (Leiden: Brill, 1986); M. K. Wakeman, *God's Battle with the Monster* (Leiden: Brill, 1973).

Page 70: "The serpent had achieved his aim." See the *Catechism of the Catholic Church:* "By our first parents' sin, the devil has acquired a certain domination over man, even though he remains free. Original sin entails 'captivity under the power of him who thenceforth had the power of death, that is, the devil'" (no. 407, citing Heb 2:14–15). "The whole of man's history has been the story of dour combat with the powers of evil. Stretching, so our Lord tells us, from the very dawn of history until the last day. Finding himself in the midst of the battlefield man has to struggle to do what is right, and it is at great cost to himself." (no. 409). Also see Robert W. L. Moberly, "Did the Serpent Get It Right?" in *From Eden to Golgotha: Essays in Biblical Theology* (Atlanta: Scholars Press, 1992), pp. 1–27.

Page 71: "Adam and Eve chose to die spiritually." On the reality of the "spiritual death" intended by the text ("die the death") and experienced by Adam and Eve, see G. J. Wenham, *Genesis 1–15* (Waco, Tex.: Word Books, 1987), p. 90: "To be expelled from the camp of Israel or to be rejected by God was to experience a living death. . . . Only in the presence of God did man enjoy fullness of life. To choose anything else is to choose death (Prov 8:36). The expulsion from the garden of delight where God himself lived would therefore have been regarded by the godly men of ancient Israel as yet more catastrophic than physical death. The latter was the ultimate sign and seal of the spiritual death the human couple experienced on the day they ate from the forbidden tree. . . . As a paradigm of sin this model would be equally at home in any of the great theological traditions of the Old Testament." A similar covenantal interpretation also fits other occurrences of this double-death formula (Hebrew, *moth tamuth;* Gn 20:7; 1 Sm 14:44; 22:16; 1 Kgs 2:37, 42; 2 Kgs 1:4, 6, 16; Jer 26:8; Ez 3:18; 33:8, 14); cf. S. Sekine, *Transcendency and Symbols in the Old Testament* (New York: Walter de Gruyter, 1999), pp. 240ff.

Page 73: "Like a riddle, the story of Adam and Eve operates on two levels." For a similar treatment of the temptation narrative in terms of a "riddle" (though with different results), see H. Blocher, *Original Sin: Illuminating the Riddle* (Grand Rapids, Mich.: Eerdmans, 1999). Blocher paraphrases St. Augustine's comment about the cause and consequence of Adam's sin: "Nothing is so easy to denounce, nothing is so difficult to understand" (p. 15). For more on the important (but neglected) use of riddles in Old Testament narrative settings, see "Riddles in the Old Testament" in J. L. Crenshaw, *Samson: A Secret Betrayed, a Vow Ignored* (Atlanta: John Knox Press, 1978), pp. 106–11. Crenshaw points out how "an ancient text (Numbers 12:8) intimates that normal revelatory discourse took place by means of riddles" (p. 106). He then examines a similar statement found in Ps 78:2, where "riddle" and "proverb" are used synonymously: "A nation recalls its weaker moments, which seem to linger in the national conscience as a kind of spiritual chastisement. . . . In it God breaks the silence of eternity and couches his speech in mystery that conceals and invites interpretation. Israel's sages saw their task as the mastering of the art of opening dark sayings" (p. 107; see Prv 1:6). Crenshaw cites the example of Solomon, whose superior wisdom was marked precisely by his uncanny ability to solve riddles (1 Kgs 10:3). Crenshaw explains: "Essential to riddles is the setting of a trap. They endeavor to mislead by offering special language that masquerades as common language" (p. 99). Significantly, Crenshaw also observes: "Double entendre, the use of double meanings, is used profusely in riddling, particularly since sex and religion constitute the two favorite topics of riddles. It follows that weddings supply a perfect occasion for the posing of riddles. . . . For such a prize, the risk of life and limb seemed a mere trifle" (p. 102). Also see J. K. A. Smith,

The Fall of Interpretation: Philosophical Foundations for a Creational Hermeneutic (Downers Grove, Ill.: InterVarsity Press, 2000).

Page 74: "Sin cuts across this one whole process . . ." R. Kehoe, O.P., "The Holy Spirit in the Scriptures," in C. Hastings and D. Nicholl, eds., *Selection II* (London: Sheed and Ward, 1954), p. 9. Kehoe shows that God's plan for creation and humankind is "that Flesh might participate in the Spirit, that nature might be transformed by the power of the Spirit," for which "nature must first die to itself." Thus, he concludes: "The Fall tells of the failure to accept the Sacrifice that this implies. . . . There must be a Wisdom . . . which knows how to die in order to find life. . . . But man rejected this way of sacrifice . . . being seduced to belief that Eros could find its fulfillment without having to die" (pp. 8, 12). See A. McGill, "Self-Giving as the Inner Life of God," in *Suffering: A Test of Theological Method* (Philadelphia: Westminster Press, 1982); M. Foss, *Death, Sacrifice, and Tragedy* (Lincoln, Nebr.: University of Nebraska Press, 1966).

Page 79: "Because of the covenants . . ." See Cross, "Kinship and Covenant," pp. 12–13: "The league in ideal form was conceived as twelve tribes, related at once by covenant and kinship. . . . Israel is the kindred ('*am*) of

Yahweh. . . . This is an old formula. But this formula must be understood as legal language, the language of kinship-in-law, or in other words, the language of covenant." On rendering of the Hebrew expression ʿ*am Yahweh* as "family/kin of Yahweh," rather than "people of God," see N. Lohfink, S.J., *Great Themes from the Old Testament* (Edinburgh: T. & T. Clark, 1982), pp. 119–32.

Page 79: "The redeeming kinsman . . ." On the family identity of the *go'el* as "kinsman-redeemer," see Cross, "Kinship and Covenant," pp. 4–5: "To the kinship group, the family *(mishpahah)*, falls the duty of redemption. . . . The duties of the *go'el* are several: to avenge the blood of a kinsman, to redeem property sold by a poor kinsman, to redeem the kinsman sold into debt slavery. . . . These laws . . . have their origin in the kinship group . . . which held property in common as an inalienable patrimony." Also see C. Stuhlmueller, C.P., *Creative Redemption in Deutero-Isaiah* (Rome: Pontifical Biblical Institute, 1970), pp. 99–131, who shows how the Hebrew term "forcefully brings out the idea of a *family or blood-bond* between the redeemer and one redeemed" (p. 100).

Page 83: "In space and time, Jesus Christ would carry out . . ." For a very profound yet accessible meditation on how the language of the Trinity's love speaks to the deepest longings of the human heart, see M. Downey, *Altogether Gift: A Trinitarian Spirituality* (Maryknoll, N.Y.: Orbis Books, 2000).

Page 84: "Being subject to perpetual bondage . . ." See C. Leget, *Living with God: Thomas Aquinas on the Relation Between Life and Earth and "Life" After Death* (Leuven, Belgium: Peeters, 1997), pp. 117–18.

Page 87: "our sublime vocation as sons in the Son." See Encyclical Letter by Pope John Paul II, *Veritatis Splendor* (The Splendor of Truth) (Boston: Pauline Books and Media, 1993), p. 31; also see M. Vellanickal, *Divine Sonship of Man in the Bible* (Kottayam, India: PSP, 1999); idem, *The Divine Sonship of Christians in the Johannine Writings* (Rome: Pontifical Biblical Institute, 1977).

Page 87: "The early Christians dared to call this process . . ." See St. Augustine *Exposition of the Psalms* 50.2; St. Gregory Nazianzen *Orations* 30.14, 38.13; St. Maximus the Confessor quoted in *The Philokalia,* vol. 2 (London: Faber and Faber, 1981), p. 171; St. Cyril of Alexandria *Commentary on John* 1.8; St. John Damascene *Orthodox Faith* 2.12, 4.13. For a contemporary account, see Christoph Cardinal Schonborn, "Is Man to Become God? On the Meaning of the Christian Doctrine of Deification," in *From Death to Life* (San Francisco: Ignatius Press, 1995), pp. 41–63.

Page 87: "It was for this end . . ." St. Irenaeus *Against the Heresies* 3.19.1.

Page 87: "We might be made God . . ." St. Athanasius *On the Incarnation* 54.3.

Page 90: "Re-flesh My Memory." On the vivid realism of "remembrance" in various liturgical passages in the Old and New Testaments, see F. Chenderlin, *"Do This as My Memorial": The Semantic and Conceptual Background of "Anamnesis" in 1 Corinthians 11:24–25* (Rome: Pontifical Biblical Institute, 1982); B. Childs, *Memory and Tradition in Israel* (London: SCM Press, 1962); M. Thurian, *The Eucharistic Memorial,* 2 vols. (Richmond, Va.: John Knox Press, 1961).

Page 92: "union with those whom He loves . . ." N. Cabasilas, *The Life in Christ* (Crestwood, N.Y.: St. Vladimir's Seminary Press, 1998), p. 46.

Page 93: "Without grace and freedom, Adam could not have truly given himself . . . and could not imitate the inner life of the Trinity." For a profoundly illuminating treatment of St. Thomas Aquinas's theological framework for understanding how Adam's voluntary offering of natural life would have perfected his supernatural life, see Leget, *Living with God,* pp. 67–268. "Thus Aquinas can state that compared to the life of grace, natural life is

almost nothing" (p. 87). "Aquinas notices that many people are more afraid of corporal than of spiritual punish-
ments. That the loss of the life of grace is infinitely more
undesirable than that of corporal life, is not evident for
those who are only familiar with the sensible and corporal goods" (p. 93). "Moreover, Aquinas takes away all
doubt that one might reach the quantity of heavenly
charity in this life: the latter is of a different order and not
a simple extrapolation of the love on earth. . . . The
virtue of charity is perfected by the gift of *sapientia*. The
gift of wisdom enables one to consider the highest cause
by which all other things can be judged and at which
they can be directed" (pp. 165–66). "This union has an
impact on the appreciation of life on earth and the atti-
tude towards one's own death. The theological virtues
display a dynamism according to which one is increas-
ingly concerned about God instead of oneself" (p. 166).
"Now, when corporal life is sacrificed for the sake of the
life of grace, natural life . . . is sacrificed. . . . Yet this is
not unreasonable: the life of grace is of infinitely greater
value than natural life. . . . The end of natural life implies
the end of the *status merendi,* the state in which man de-
velops his relationship with God through moral action. . . . Thus, this act of faith, hope and charity is
ultimately eschatological and the greatest expression of
love for and confidence in God that can be thought of.
In the action of the martyr the highest degree of
charity . . . is directly related to the greatest sign of love

one can exhibit for one's neighbor (Jn 15:13). This action of highest perfection is to be recognized as the work of the Spirit: an invisible mission or new inhabitation in the human soul. By giving up one's corporal life in this manner, one directly enters the life of God" (pp. 179–80).

Page 99: "For us mere mortals . . ." J. A. DiNoia, O.P., "Moral Life as Transfigured Life," in J. A. DiNoia, O.P., and R. Cessario, O.P., eds., *Veritatis Splendor and the Renewal of Moral Theology* (Chicago: Midwest Theological Forum, 1999), p. 5.

Page 99: "With Baptism we become children . . ." See Apostolic Exhortation by Pope John Paul II, *Christifideles Laici* (The Lay Members of Christ's Faithful People) (Boston: St. Paul Books and Media, 1988), p. 28.

Page 100: "Let us rejoice and give thanks . . ." *Christifideles Laici,* p. 43, quoting St. Augustine *Tractates on the Gospel of John* 21.8.

Page 106: "The willingness to serve . . ." St. Cyril of Alexandria *Commentary on the Gospel of St. Luke.*

Page 107: "By this arrangement . . ." St. Irenaeus *Against the Heresies* 4.38.3.

Page 116: "Throughout his letters, St. Paul used two images . . ." P. Andriessen, O.S.B., "The New Eve, Body of the New Adam," in J. Giblet et al., *The Birth of the Church: A Biblical Study* (Staten Island, N.Y.: Alba House, 1968), pp. 111–39; C. Chavasse, *The Bride of Christ: An Enquiry into the Nuptial Element in Early Christianity* (London: Religious Book Club, 1939).

Page 117: "Lady Mother Church," Tertullian *Ad martyras* 1. See J. C. Plumpe, *Mater Ecclesia: An Inquiry into the Concept of the Church as Mother in Early Christianity* (Washington, D.C.: Catholic University of America Press, 1943).

Page 117: "He cannot have God for His Father . . ." St. Cyprian *The Unity of the Church* 6.

Page 117: "She is one mother, plentiful in fruitfulness." St. Cyprian *The Unity of the Church* 5.

Page 118: "In the supernatural family of the saints . . ." See S. Hahn, *Hail, Holy Queen: The Mother of God in the Word of God* (New York: Doubleday, 2001).

Page 120: "They replaced the portraits . . ." Dom Gregory Dix, *The Shape of the Liturgy* (London: A. & C. Black, 1945), p. 27.

Page 121: "the great family which is the Church . . ." See Pope John Paul II, *Familiaris Consortio* (The role of the Christian family in the modern world) (Boston: Daughters of St. Paul, 1981), p. 128. For the prevalence of familial images in the theological teachings of Vatican II, see Augustin Cardinal Bea, *The Church and Mankind* (Chicago: Franciscan Herald Press, 1967).

Page 123: "Be obedient to your bishop . . ." St. Ignatius of Antioch *Letter to the Magnesians* 13; *Letter to the Ephesians* 5; St. Jerome *Epist.* 3 (PG, 46:1024); St. Augustine *In Psalm.* 44.32 (CCL, 38:516); all cited by Henri Cardinal de Lubac, S.J., "The Fatherhood of the Clergy," in *The Motherhood of the Church* (San Francisco: Ignatius Press, 1982), pp. 85–97. De Lubac also shows how, in the early Church Fathers, "the authority of the bishop has an essentially paternal character. If he is the head, it is because he is father" (p. 105).

Page 127: "the Great Unknown." B1. J. Escriva de Balaguer, "The Great Unknown," homily in *Christ Is Passing By* (Chicago: Scepter, 1973), pp. 173–87.

Page 131: "Speaking Words of Wisdom." See T. P. McCreesh, O.P., "Wisdom as Wife," *Revue Biblique* 92 (1985): 25–46. For a penetrating treatment of the key text, Wis 7–9, see J. L. Crenshaw, *Old Testament Wisdom,* rev. ed. (Louisville, Ky.: Westminster John Knox Press,

1998), p. 199: "A further step is taken in Wisdom of Solomon 7–9, one that is bold beyond belief. True, she is a personification, with its erotic overtones, which occur in reference to Solomon's bride, wisdom, but chapter 7 describes her as an extension of divine essence, a virtual if not actual hypostasis. Her twenty-one attributes add up to supreme purity, an emanation of the glory of the Almighty, and an image of divine goodness (7:22–26). Divine wisdom and spirit unite, and wisdom functions as a providential power at work in the life of the covenantal people."

Page 132: "Benedict Ashley, O.P., notices how Wisdom . . ." B. Ashley, O.P., *Justice in the Church: Gender and Participation* (Washington, D.C.: Catholic University of America Press, 1996), p. 116. Ashley adds, "Thus, although the Holy Spirit, as all the Divine Persons, is named as masculine, the church to which as its very soul the Spirit gives life is feminine and complements Christ as his Bride. Therefore, it is in the covenant relation of the church to Christ, in their union of love, that the Holy Spirit is especially revealed" (p. 117).

Page 132: "Another common Old Testament image . . ." See Fishbane, *Kiss of God,* pp. 107–8, 111–12; R. Patai, *The Hebrew Goddess,* 3rd ed. (Detroit: Wayne State University, 1990), pp. 96–111.

Page 133: "As the soul is in our body . . ." See Encyclical Letter by Pope Leo XIII, *Divinum Illud Munus* (On the Holy Spirit), 6 quoting St. Augustine *Sermon* 267.4; also see de Lubac, *Motherhood of the Church,* p. 117: "The hierarchical Church is 'pneumatic' as well: it is the Spirit sent by Jesus who animates her." Also see M. J. Scheeben, *Mariology,* vol. 1 (St. Louis: Herder, 1946), p. 170, and the *Catechism of the Catholic Church,* nos. 797–98.

Page 133: "The soul forms the body . . ." Pope John Paul II, *Original Unity of Man and Woman,* p. 109.

Page 134: "masculine" or "feminine" qualities: See Pope John Paul II, *Mulieris Dignitatem (On the Dignity and Vocation of Women)* (Boston: St. Paul Books, 1988), p. 31: "This characteristic of biblical language—its anthropomorphic way of speaking about God—points indirectly to the mystery of the eternal 'generating' which belongs to the inner life of God. Nevertheless, in itself this 'generating' has neither 'masculine' nor 'feminine' qualities. It is by nature totally divine. It is spiritual in the most perfect way, since 'God is spirit' (Jn 4:24) and possesses no property typical of the body, neither 'feminine' nor 'masculine.' Thus even 'fatherhood' in God is completely divine and free of the 'masculine' bodily characteristics proper to human fatherhood."

Also see John S. Grabowski, "Theological Anthropology and Gender Since Vatican II: A Critical Appraisal of Recent Trends in Catholic Theology" (Ph.D. Dissertation, Marquette University, 1991), p. 374: "To say that the Holy Spirit is the locus of feminine and maternal qualities within the Godhead is not to give the Spirit corporeality or sexuality any more than the paternity of the Father or the filiation of the Son gives them these characteristics. The Holy Spirit actualizes these qualities in a divine and spiritual way. Furthermore, since the Spirit proceeds from the Father and the Son but does not cause them in turn, there can be no misreading of the Trinitarian processions in pagan terms of sexual union or generation. The maintenance of the order of these Trinitarian processions equally excludes the pagan confusion of God with the world. . . . The Spirit may be immanent within the world leading humanity to Christ and through him to the Father, but neither the Spirit nor the other divine Persons are identified with the world. Rather, in their complete possession of the one divine nature the three divine Persons infinitely transcend the world even while being intimately related to it as cause and ground. More work is needed to examine the adequacy of such a description of the Holy Spirit in feminine terms . . . [S]uch a view can be maintained only as a theological hypothesis in need of further refinement and research."

Page 134: "Cardinal Yves M. J. Congar saw this . . ." Y. M. J. Congar, *I Believe in the Holy Spirit,* vol. 3 (New York: Seabury, 1985), p. 155; idem, "The Spirit as God's Femininity," *Theology Digest* 30 (1982): 129–32.

Page 135: "No less a doctrinal authority than . . ." Joseph Cardinal Ratzinger, *Daughter Zion* (San Francisco: Ignatius Press, 1983), pp. 26–27. See B. Albrecht, "Is There an Objective Type 'Woman'?" in H. Moll, J. Ratzinger, et al., eds., *The Church and Women* (San Francisco: Ignatius Press, 1988), p. 48: "Father Kentenich [founder of the Schoenstatt Movement], decades before the current debate . . . perceived in the Holy Spirit the deepest mysteries . . . of God and woman in each other. The Holy Spirit (not Mary) is the 'feminine dimension of God,' if one may use such language in a hypothesis not sufficiently refined. Mary is, in her graced humanity, the instrument of the Holy Spirit." See L. Bouyer, *Women in the Church* (San Francisco: Ignatius Press, 1979), pp. 37–39; idem, *The Seat of Wisdom* (New York: Pantheon Books, 1960), pp. 175–90; P. Gadenz, "The Church as the Family of God," in Hahn and Suprenant, eds., *Catholic for a Reason,* pp. 73–75.

Page 135: "In fact, some of the greatest of the ancient Fathers . . ." See J. Chalassery, *The Holy Spirit and Christian Initiation in the East Syrian Tradition* (Rome: Mar Thoma Yogam, 1995), p. 188: "In the East Syrian sources the motherhood of the Church was diminished due to the motherhood of the Holy Spirit. . . . Therefore, we can interpret the Church as the visible image of the motherhood of the Holy Spirit. The Holy Spirit is the power behind all the motherly actions of the Church." Elsewhere he adds, "The Holy Spirit acts as mother in the life of Christians. . . . Aphrahat, in his Demonstration *On Virginity,* says: 'When a man has not yet taken a wife, he loves and honors God, his Father, and the Holy Spirit, his Mother.' . . . in the rites of Christian Initiation, it is the Holy Spirit who gives birth to Christians in the Church through the womb of baptism. As a mother the Spirit prepares spiritual food for 'her' children. . . . Therefore, Narsai says: 'They suck the Spirit after the birth of Baptism'" (pp. 233–34, citing Narsai *Liturgical Homilies* 21.52–55). Also see S. Harvey, "Feminine Imagery for the Divine: The Holy Spirit, the Odes of Solomon, and Early Syriac Tradition," *St. Vladimir's Theological Quarterly* 37 (1993): 111–39.

Page 135: "St. Methodius of Olympus saw this . . ." See M. J. Scheeben, *The Mysteries of Christianity* (St. Louis: Herder, 1946), p. 185: "As Eve can, in a figurative sense, be called simply the rib of Adam, since she was formed from the rib of Adam, St. Methodius goes so far as to assert that the Holy Spirit is the *costa Verbi.* . . . 'By the rib,' says St. Methodius, 'we rightly understand the Paraclete, the Spirit of truth . . . quite properly called the rib of the

Logos'" (citing *Convivius decem virginum* III.C.8; PG, 18:73). Also see R. Murray, S.J., *Symbols of Church and Kingdom: A Study in Early Syriac Tradition* (New York: Cambridge University Press, 1977), p. 318: "It is not said of Eve that she was Adam's sister or his daughter, but that she came from him; likewise it is not to be said that the Spirit is a daughter or a sister, but that [she] is *from* God and consubstantial with him" (citing St. Ephrem *Evangelium concordans* 19.15; CSCO, 137). Also see M. D. Torre, "St. John Damascene and St. Thomas Aquinas on the Eternal Procession of the Holy Spirit," *St. Vladimir's Theological Quarterly* 38 (1994): 303–27; D. Belonick, "Father, Son, and Spirit—So What's in a Name?" in H. H. Hitchcock, ed., *The Politics of Prayer: Feminist Language and the Worship of God* (San Francisco: Ignatius Press, 1992), p. 305: "the Fathers compared the procession of the Holy Spirit . . . with the 'procession' of Eve from Adam. Later, in the seventh century, Anastasius of Sinai wrote: 'Eve, who proceeded from Adam, signifies the proceeding Person of the Holy Spirit. This is why God did not breathe in her the breath of life; she was already the type of the breathing and life of the Holy Spirit *(On the Image and Likeness).*' "

Page 136: "The Holy Spirit becomes . . ." St. Catherine of Siena *Dialogues* 141.

Page 136: "St. Maximilian Kolbe . . ." H. M. Manteau-Bonamy, *The Immaculate Conception and the*

Holy Spirit: The Marian Teachings of Father Kolbe (San Francisco: Ignatius Press, 1988), p. 68. Elsewhere, Kolbe writes, "The Holy Spirit is, therefore, the uncreated eternal conception, the prototype of all conceptions that multiply life throughout the universe. The Father begets; the Son is begotten; the Spirit is the 'conception' that springs from their love" (cited by Most Rev. D. Montrose, Bishop of Stockton, in "The Message of the Virgin of Lourdes," *Spes Nostra* 4 [1996]: 5).

Page 136: "uncreated immaculate conception . . ." Manteau-Bonamy, *Immaculate Conception,* p. 3.

Page 136: "quasi-incarnatus . . ." Manteau-Bonamy, *Immaculate Conception,* p. 96. The "quasi" is what salvages this expression, since the Spirit and Mary are not united "hypostatically," but as two distinct persons, one divine and the other human. More preferable, perhaps, is the notion of Mary as "icon" or "created replication" of the Holy Spirit. For some profoundly illuminating work in this area of biblical theology, see F. X. Durrwell, *Mary: Icon of the Spirit and of the Church* (Middlegreen, U.K.: St. Paul Publications, 1990); idem, *The Spirit of the Father and of the Son* (Middlegreen, U.K.: St. Paul Publications, 1989); idem, *Holy Spirit of God: An Essay in Biblical Theology* (London: Geoffrey Chapman, 1986); A. Feuillet, *Jesus and His Mother: The Role of the Virgin Mary in Salvation History and the Place of Woman in the Church* (Still River, Mass.: St. Bede's Publications, 1984), pp. 209–12.

Page 136: "Another recent witness . . ." B1. E. Stein, *Essays on Woman* (Washington, D.C.: ICS, 1987), vol. 2 of *Collected Works,* p. 191.

Page 137: "the Hebrew word for 'marriage' is *kiddushin . . .*" See S. Rosenberg, *Judaism* (New York: Paulist, 1966), p. 118: "For all Jews marriage is a sacred act and for that reason it is called *kiddushin,* or sanctification." Also see Schillebeeckx, *Marriage,* p. 100; J. Mohler, S.J., *Love, Marriage and the Family* (Staten Island, N.Y.: Alba House, 1982), p. 26. On the symbolic meaning of "unveiling" for the act of consummation (at the climax of a seven-day ceremony) in ancient Judaism, see Gn 29:21–30; Jgs 14:10–20; J. L. McKenzie, *Dictionary of the Bible* (Milwaukee: Bruce, 1965), p. 912: "the veil was worn by women at the time of marriage and at the consummation of the marriage." Also see R. Patai, *Family, Love and the Bible* (London: MacGibbon and Kee, 1960), pp. 58–59.

Page 137: "The Spirit and the Bride say, 'Come!' " For an insightful treatment of this passage, see J. Corbon, O.P., *The Wellspring of Worship* (New York: Paulist Press, 1988), pp. 53–54: "Now the final vision of the Apocalypse reveals its full meaning. . . . the vision has to do with the betrothed, the bride of the Lamb. After all, it is precisely in order to show her to him that the angel has carried John in spirit to the top of a high mountain. . . . But then, at the end, at the very moment the mystery is entirely unveiled in sober symbols, we no longer see her. It is the river of life that fills the horizon. What, then, is this energy, this crystal-clear water? It is the only presence that cannot be named and that makes itself known in the utter transparency of the Bride: it is the Spirit. . . . In this light-filled silence in which the vision of the Church of the last times culminates, the angel seems to whisper to John the Theologian: 'You have seen the Bride of the Lamb? You have seen the Spirit!' . . . The one whom the Theologian contemplates is the Bride of the Lamb, and in her he reveals to us the kenosis of the Spirit. . . . The fact that the Bride is transparent for the Spirit to shine through is explicable only because she is the living locus of the kenosis of the Holy Spirit. And she herself shares in that kenosis because it is what makes her the Bride of the Lamb. . . . Just as Mary in becoming Mother of the Word incarnate began the fullness of time in her own person by the energy of the Holy Spirit, so too . . . the Church becomes bride and mother through the Spirit of Jesus who dwells in her. This, then, is the last times: the Spirit and the Bride." Elsewhere, Corbon describes the Church's liturgy as "the overflow of his life-giving Spirit," whom he describes as "the maternal envoy of the Father" and "the Father's passionate love for his Son and for all his children" (pp.

64–65). Significantly, Corbon was the only nonbishop directly entrusted, by Cardinals Ratzinger and Schonborn, with the responsibility to draft sections of the original text of the *Catechism of the Catholic Church*. Not surprisingly, then, many of these points are echoed there (see "The Holy Spirit and the Church in the Liturgy," nos. 1091–1139; also see nos. 2642–55).

Page 138: "By divine actions that are bridal and maternal . . ." The best treatment is still Scheeben's (*Mariology*, vol. 1, pp. 154–218). He shows how Mary's title "spouse of the Spirit" may be properly understood, without being determinative of the Spirit's personhood, in any way. Indeed, the eternal personhood of the Spirit cannot be made to depend on a creature, no matter how exalted (e.g., Mary), since that would imply absurd or impossible notions (viz., before Mary's creation, the Trinity would have consisted of a Father, Son, and Holy *Bachelor*).

Page 139: "The first Person knows Himself . . ." F. Sheed, *Theology and Sanity* (San Francisco: Ignatius Press, 1993), p. 106. Some versions of the "social analogy" of the Trinity are advanced without adequate regard to the spiritual nature of the divine processions, which the "psychological analogy" is better equipped to safeguard; e.g., C. Plantinga, "Social Trinity and Tritheism," in C. Plantinga and R. Feenstra, eds., *Trinity, Incarnation and*

Atonement (Notre Dame, Ind.: Notre Dame University Press, 1989), pp. 21–47. A thoughtful critique is offered by B. Leftow, "Anti Social Trinitarianism," in S. David et al., eds., *The Trinity* (New York: Oxford University Press, 1999), pp. 203–49. One underlying problem is the modern tendency to neglect family relations (e.g., fatherhood, sonship, bridal-maternity) in favor of physical gender (male, female). For an interesting study that traces the modern intellectual habit of thinking of relations in individualistic terms of sex and gender all the way back to the European Enlightenment, and its fixation with conceptual abstractions, see I. Illich, *Gender* (New York: Pantheon Books, 1982). He contrasts this modern approach with the greater realism of premodern societies, which tended to treat persons in more relational terms; i.e., daughters and sons are what we are at birth, not merely females and males. Also see H. T. Wilson, *Sex and Gender: Making Cultural Sense of Civilization* (Leiden: Brill, 1989).

Page 141: "We can describe our sanctification . . ." See A. Nachef, *Mary's Pope: John Paul II, Mary, and the Church Since Vatican II* (Franklin, Wis.: Sheed and Ward, 2000), p. 103: "The Holy Spirit connects not only the motherhood of Mary at the Annunciation and her motherhood in the order of grace but also the virginal motherhood of God with the virginal motherhood of the Church. . . . That the Holy Spirit is the Divine Person who assures the continuity between the virginal motherhood of Mary and the virginal motherhood of the Church is a fact that has become a pattern in the Pneumatology of Pope John Paul II."

Pages 142: "If the man is the head . . ." Encyclical by Pope Pius XI, *Casti Connubii* (On Christian marriage) (Boston: Daughters of St. Paul, 1930), p. 15. See J. Grabowski, "Mutual Submission and Trinitarian Self-Giving," *Angelicum* 74 (1997): 504–5: "Hence as the Holy Spirit is the bond of love and communion within trinitarian life, so it can be suggested that women analogically reflect and embody the same qualities in nurturing and sustaining communion within marriage and the family." Also see P. F. de Solenni, *A Hermeneutic of Aquinas's "Mens" Through a Sexually Differentiated Epistemology: Towards an Understanding of Woman as Imago Dei* (Rome: Apollinare Studi, 2000); J. Hartel, *Femina ut Imago Dei: The Integral Feminism of St. Thomas Aquinas* (Rome: Pontifical Gregorian University, 1993).

Page 143: "To be fully human, to be fully divinized . . ." See de Margerie, *Christian Trinity in History,* pp. 287–88: "The family analogy of the Trinity can be broken up into two aspects: the paternity-filiation aspect and the conjugal aspect. . . . It seems to us then that a great part of the difficulties that have for so long a time been urged against the explication of the conjugal dimension of the family analogy have disappeared today. We think the moment has come to deepen this analogy. . . . The inner logic of the New Testament does more than authorize such a conclusion. It demands it." See W. D. Virtue, *Mother and Infant: The Moral Theology of Embodied Self-Giving in Motherhood* (Rome: Pontifical University of St. Thomas, 1995); E. C. Muller, *Trinity and Marriage in Paul* (New York: Peter Lang, 1990).

Page 149: "look upon one who looks back in love." St. Augustine *Sermon* 69.2–3.

Page 164: "Original sin is not only . . ." Pope John Paul II, *Crossing the Threshold of Hope* (New York: Alfred A. Knopf, 1994), p. 228.

Page 164: "They have a number of rock-solid reasons . . ." Some material here is adapted from Hahn, "Mystery of the Family of God," in Hahn and Suprenant, eds., *Catholic for a Reason,* pp. 15–18.

Page 170: "Remember, the Latin word for 'oath' is *sacramentum* . . ." See H. O. Old, *Themes and Variations for a Christian Doxology: Some Thoughts on the Theology of Worship* (Grand Rapids, Mich.: Eerdmans, 1992), p. 119: "When Tertullian calls baptism a *sacramentum* . . . the very choice of that word implies a covenantal understanding of worship." For an approach similar to mine, only from Protestant perspectives, see J. F. White, *Sacraments as God's Self-Giving* (Nashville: Abingdon Press, 1983); M. G. Kline, *By Oath Consigned: A Reinterpretation of the Covenant Signs of Circumcision and Baptism* (Grand Rapids, Mich.: Eerdmans, 1968).